Heart of the
Somerset & Dorset Railway

To Graham
my very best
Wishes

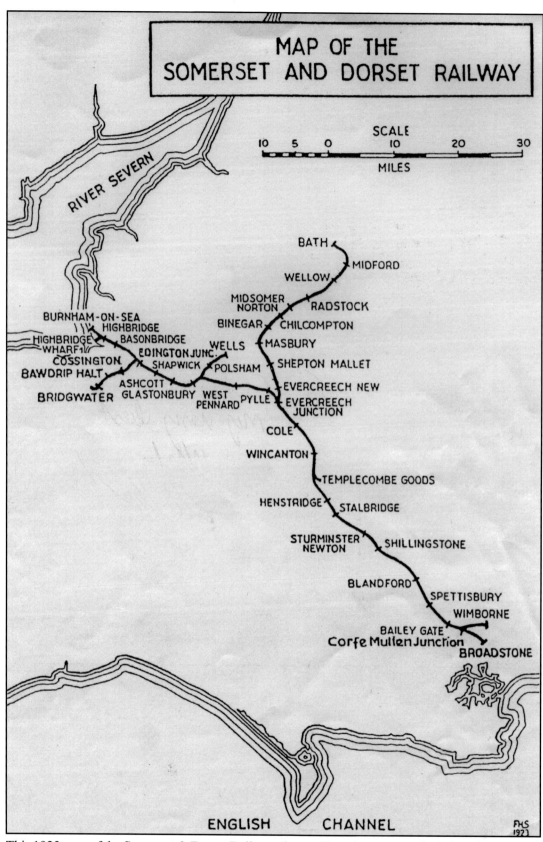

This 1923 map of the Somerset & Dorset Railway shows all stations except the halts of Stourpaine & Durweston, Charlton Marshall, Corfe Mullen, which all opened in 1928, and Shoscombe & Single Hill, which opened in 1929. (*by courtesy of the Somerset & Dorset Railway Trust*)

Heart of the
Somerset & Dorset Railway

Alan Hammond

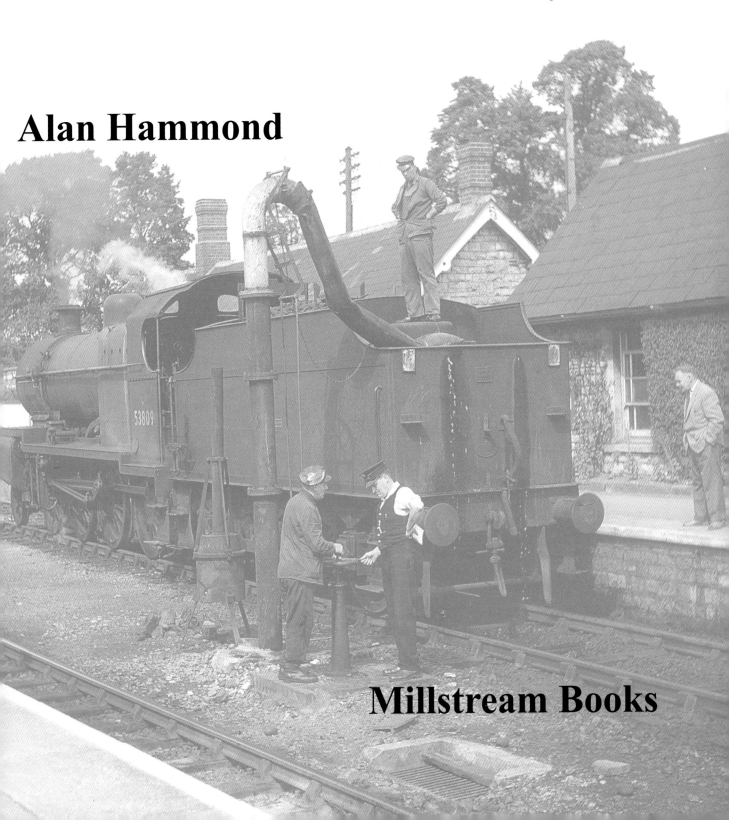

Millstream Books

This book is dedicated to
Mike Palmer
who passed away on 27 May 1999.
Mike joined the S&D Railway Circle in 1967, which later became the Somerset & Dorset Railway Trust.
Mike was the secretary, driving force and heart of the SDRT. His dedication, enthusiasm and energy made sure the
Trust went from strength to strength. His love and passion for railways, especially the S&D, was self-evident.
Mike's personality and presence in working with others to get the job done was legendary.
His memory will live on in the folklore of the Railway Preservation Movement.

Caricature of Vic Freak at Evercreech New
station drawn by stationmaster Reg Jeans.

First published in 2002 by
Millstream Books, 18 The Tyning, Bath BA2 6AL

Set in Times New Roman and printed in Great Britain by
The Amadeus Press, Cleckheaton, West Yorkshire

© Alan Hammond 2002

ISBN 0 948975 64 4

British Library Cataloguing-in-Publication Data:
a catalogue record for this book is available from the British Library

Foreword

I can't remember a time when music and railways were not the main interests of my life. Little did I realise when watching the last years of the London & North Western engines in 1949, on the railway by the side of my house, that railways, and particularly the London & North Western, would play such an important part in my life.

It seemed quite impossible, during those hectic train-spotting years of the 50s, that I might end up owning some of these wondrous machines. I have been lucky enough through the 35 years of writing hits for stars such as Kylie, Jason, Rick Astley and Steps to take part in probably one of the greatest tributes to the Industrial Age – 'Preservation'.

I spent most of my early childhood roaming the West Country with my parents searching for engines I had not seen before. Our car, which was an Austin 8, seemed only to find Minehead, which became a favourite spotting site. I travelled the Somerset and Dorset, only a few times, but their engines were always of a fascination to me, seeing many of them at Bath Green Park. I can always recall seeing a *Trains Illustrated* article of the early 50s trains on the Somerset and Dorset. It introduced many young enthusiasts to the line.

Alan's new book, *Heart of the Somerset & Dorset Railway,* and his series of other books on the S&D are a fitting tribute to the people who worked on it and the railway itself. One can sit and wonder what if? Along with these books and the footage that survives via numerous enthusiasts, few railways can claim the genuine affection that this one receives.

As we entered the new millennium some of our beloved steam engines approached their 100 years; even engines built during the early BR period are now approaching their 50th year. Let us not only enjoy the reminiscing of former railwaymen and books dedicated to them, but enjoy the Indian summer of steam.

Pete Waterman 2002

Introduction & Acknowledgements

The Somerset & Dorset Railway always evokes people's passions about the steam era. The line ran from Bath to Bournemouth, travelling through beautiful countryside and ending up at the seaside, with the added attraction of meandering across the Somerset levels from Evercreech Junction to Burnham-on-Sea, with branch lines to Wells and Bridgwater. Hopefully this new book will rekindle those bygone days. To many people who worked on the S&D it wasn't just a job, it was a way of life, both for them and for their families before them. They were proud to have been associated with the S&D and still are.

In this volume I have tried to combine all aspects of the S&D with many previously unseen photographs. There is also a selection of memories by people who worked and travelled on this most famous of lines.

I am indebted to so many people whose knowledge and kindness has been overwhelming in the writing of this book. I would especially like to offer my thanks to Pete Waterman for writing the foreword; also to my publisher, Tim Graham, for his encouragement and design skills. Very special thanks must go to Keith Barrett who has allowed me to choose photographs, luggage labels and tickets from his vast S&D collection. He has also been of immense help with constructive and helpful comments, whilst proofreading this book, as have Roy Pitman, John Simms, Christine Hammond, Irene Hammond, Cliff Smith, Gordon Hatcher, Roy Miles, Andy Moon and Richard Derry.

My sincere thanks go to all the contributors of stories and photographs and to Tony Pitt for his superb poem.

Many other people have helped in different ways. I am most grateful to Stuart Mullins, John Lock, Des Lock, Paul Fry, Norman Cook, Maurice Cook, Terry Fry, Chris Handley, Tim Deacon, Terry Loader, George Thomas, Reg Biffin, Richard Gunning, Geoffrey Wheeler, Trevor Jeans, Jack Hobbs, Ian Matthews, Chris Dyer, Alan Grieve, Dennis Ashill, Pat Bean, Fred Lester, Percy Parsons, Tony & Janet Rossiter, Frank Staddon, John Stamp, Mona Pitman, Vic Freak, Bob Downes, Mike Beale, John Rice, Ron Snook, Norman Rallison, Rodney Scovell, Betty Spiller, Brian Winter, David Milton, Mary Draper, Tony Ward and Laurie Poulton. Thanks also go to the Somerset & Dorset Railway Trust for allowing me access to their photographic collection, so professionally put together by Jason Baker.

As many photographs are from the collections of S&D staff, a reader may well recognise a photograph that he or she took. In this case, I offer my apologies in advance for not being able to credit you in person.

It is always with regret when former staff pass away. Recently we have lost Gerald Trowbridge, Merv Harwood, Ken Burrows, Howard Luxon, Ted Battersby, Betty Cox (nee Simms), Ray Coates, Reg Burt, Ron Fudge, Eric Powell, Fred Epps and Harry Sneade.

Last, but not least, my thanks go to my wife and best friend Christine whose computer skills have been of immense help to me. Her loyal support since my introduction in 1989 to the S&D by my good friend Roy Pitman, has been a major factor in all of my books on the Somerset & Dorset Railway.   Alan Hammond, Minehead, 2002

It could have been so different if Pete Waterman had discovered our group, *Quota Plus*, in the 1970s. The line-up, from left to right, is Dave Buthlay, Brian Rowland, the author (note the tank top) and Dave Hughes. (*Author's collection*)

(*above*) A picture taken back in time of a group of cleaners and footplate men at Bath Green Park in the early 1900s. In the back row, second and third left, are Bill Gunning and Arthur Tidball. (*Desmond Tidball collection*)

(*left*) Restaurant room assistant Joan Miles awaiting the Pines Express at Bath Green Park in the 1950s. Joan used to serve tea in the buffet to Roy, an S&D guard. They were married in 1953 and enjoyed many years of happiness until Joan sadly passed away in 1987. (*Roy Miles*)

(*next page*) A busy scene on the coal stage (No.2 road) at Bath, c.1930, as six members of staff get LMS 2P No.634 ready for the journey south. Note the S&D No.45 still on the smokebox door. (*H.C.Casserley*)

(*above*) A footplate team photo taken in front of Ivatt class 2MT No.41242 in 1950. From left to right, Harry Waldron, Ron Gray, Doug Farrent, Roy Williams, Frank Eyles and sitting in the wheelbarrow Gordon Cross. Was this really 52 years ago? (*Roy Williams*)

Bath Green Park fireman David Norman on the footplate in the 1960s. (*George Tucker collection*)

Ivatt 2MT No. 41290 is silhouetted by sunlight in Green Park shed just after closure. (*Martyn Burch*)

John Sawyer

As a young boy in the 1950s, I lived with my parents at Odd Down in Bath. From a playing field close to where we lived I was able to look over the beautiful city. At the age of ten I first noticed steam trains leaving Bath Green Park station, making their way up through Oldfield Park before disappearing into a tunnel, and from then on I wanted to know more about this railway. I discovered books at school containing information about Bath Green Park and the history of the S&D. I became an ardent trainspotter and knew that when I left school I wanted to work on the S&D.

In 1961, three weeks after my 15th birthday, I started at Bath as an engine cleaner; I reported to foreman Fred Holmes. As expected, new boys tended to get all the messy jobs and I always seemed to have a broom in my hand or oil on my hands. There were about ten engine cleaners at that time; names I recall were Dave Norman, Chris Fell, Roger Eames, Derek Coles, Tony Pitt, Colin Powis and Albert Parsons. There were other jobs around the shed, such as stocking up the coal fire in the engine crew's mess room, keeping the sand house topped up or painting the

locos' buffers for special duties. If the call boy wasn't around the drivers would send you over to the local shop in Brougham Hayes on the Lower Bristol Road for 20 Woodbines, cakes or a paper. I never used to mind though as there was a pretty girl working in the hairdressers nearby.

Having been on the railway about nine months I started asking myself when it was going to be my chance to step up on the footplate? In June 1962 I dispensed with my engine cleaner's status and attended Mutual Improvement classes with Inspector McCarthy. Even though I wanted to be a fireman I wasn't exactly looking forward to these classes as Mac, as he was called, had a reputation of frightening some of his pupils. The idea was to learn all about the workings of the steam loco, frames, cylinders, steam chest, wheel arrangements, boilers, firebox, and of course the rule book, especially rule 55 – the protection of a train. The fireman usually carried out this duty, if a train was held at a stop signal. The driver or fireman then had to proceed to the signalbox after waiting two minutes to remind the signalman where the train had been stopped.

I was thinking to myself that this wasn't going to be very pleasant, stopped a mile or so from the nearest box, or even up on the Mendip hills in a rainstorm or surrounded by thick fog. I could imagine my driver waving me goodbye from a warm cab as I disappeared into the darkness. One day in class Mac asked: 'What is the most important item on the footplate?' One bright spark answered, 'the tea can'. We all had a good laugh except Mac. I passed the test and became a passed cleaner. My first firing turn was taking coal empties to Writhlington and Midsomer Norton.

By the time the autumn of 1962 was approaching I had been on various trips. The working times played havoc with my social life, especially the early turn. I wasn't so keen getting out of a warm bed at two in the morning especially during the winter months. My dad, being the person he was, would get out of his bed and take me to work in his old Ford Popular at these very awkward times. Later that year and at the beginning of 1963 I was to experience about the worst winter I can remember. I recall being on duty at about 08.00 on 3 January; the snow had been falling since the previous evening and there were reports on the radio of heavy drifting on the Mendip hills. On arrival at work I quickly found out that the early goods train had run into one of these drifts. Being only 16 I wasn't really aware of the danger that the train crew of driver Fred Love, fireman Tony Pitt and guard Fred Nowell were in. Later on however we found out the drift they were in was near Winsor Hill Tunnel. All trains that went beyond Midsomer Norton were cancelled, but the powers that be decided perhaps trains could run as far as Norton though eventually everything during that morning was cancelled except a hastily arranged snowplough. About 10.00 that morning I was assigned to work on one of these ploughs on an 8F. After leaving for the Mendips we were stopped at Radstock and told to return to Bath as the weather was worsening. When I returned on the same turn the next day the S&D was still closed and remained closed for a further two days. The crew stuck on the early goods were rescued many hours later with Fred Love suffering frostbite.

When spring arrived I was moved up to another link with my first regular driver Dennis Latham. Most young firemen must have fired for him at some stage during their first year. Dennis was rather a large chap and there were some turns, with small engines and small seats, when I often wondered how he was able to fit his large frame into the cab let alone the seat. One of these turns was a local passenger train, the 18.05 return to Binegar stopping at

all stations (Ivo Peters enjoyed riding on this train as a birthday treat each year). When stopping at Midsomer Norton, there was always a regular young lady passenger about my age disembarking and I always got a nice smile.

As I recall in the late summer of 1963 things began to change a little; the Western Region was beginning to gain control at Bath Green Park and the timetable was being cut bit by bit, including the freight. I was now working with driver Albert Williams, a fairly quiet man with a reputation of liking his footplate kept clean. I didn't mind this at all because I also liked the footplate to be clean. I remember being asked to work a rest day on a relief duty starting at 07.00. About half an hour later the foreman entered the engine crew's messroom looking for me. I was making a second cup of tea when he told me to throw it away as a fireman at Radstock shed had failed to arrive for his shunting turn. I was to catch the next train and undertake his duties for the day. The driver Frank Kemp was waiting eagerly for me; he had prepared our loco which was a Jinty, the normal type of engine for shunting coal out of Writhlington colliery. We went about the day's task of retrieving about ten loaded coal wagons per trip from the pit. All went well until about mid morning when lo and behold the Jinty left the track near Writhlington signalbox. After a few minutes I got the feeling that this had happened before, because the driver, guard, shunters and myself were gathering as many wooden sleepers as we could find. Of course I was only doing as I was told, but really I hadn't a clue what was going on. Working as a team we spaced these sleepers all around the loco, while Frank Kemp edged her up onto the track. We were working again within a couple of hours. When leaving to go back home I was sworn not to tell a soul about the incident to the chaps at Bath.

At Bath Green Park there were plenty of jokers and one in particular who comes to mind is driver Reg Beesley. Anyone who was at Green Park could probably tell his own version of what he used to get up to. If you were working a train in the opposite direction it could turn out to be a bit of a nightmare. Sometimes a bucket of water with some nasty contents in it would come your way, or a bundle of oily rags land in your lap. Most crews had a sense of humour so they came to accept Reg's little jokes.

As the summer of 1964 approached I had been with many drivers. One character was Ernie (Bunny) Hemmings. I remember working as his fireman on a passenger train down to Templecombe and unbeknown to me, Bunny liked his cider. On arrival at Templecombe Upper station there was a Templecombe crew waiting to relieve us to take the train on to Bournemouth. We walked the short distance to Templecombe Lower shed and the messroom for our sandwich and a fresh can of tea. We must only have been in there a matter of minutes when Bunny started to move: 'Come on kid, let's go.' 'Where' I asked? 'You'll see when we get there.' As we walked into *The Royal Hotel* I had the feeling Bunny had been here before. I had some local cider, which I didn't like, but Bunny did and enjoyed a couple of pints. I'm not sure how long we were in there, but on arrival at Templecombe station our train was waiting and so were the crew. I jumped on the Standard class 4 and got on with the job. I didn't have much to drink and really Bunny hadn't either, but he wasn't walking very straight on the way back from the pub. Leaving Templecombe was okay and I felt fine, the engine was steaming well on the flat to Evercreech and with three coaches there was not much weight behind us. We were going at some speed as we approached Midford and it's a good job we had the Whitaker apparatus attached to our Standard 4 because we whipped through there pretty fast. On arrival at Bath Green Park all I can remember Bunny saying with a grin on his face was that 'the journey went quick'. I just smiled and said, 'Yes it did'.

Apart from the different characters on the footplate there were also a few guards that had their own S&D personalities. There was Jack Frapwell otherwise known as Farmer Frapwell to us footplate crews. The first time I met Jack he was different to say the least; the first thing I noticed were his long jack boots covered in what looked like farm manure, a sort of guard's uniform with bits of string holding everything up and a pipe stuck firmly in his mouth. Over a period of time during the summer of 1964 I came in contact with Jack quite a lot and found out he had a smallholding, hence the farmyard appearance. Another well-known guard was Frank Staddon (his brother Reg was a shunter at Green Park). Frank always had a story to tell and was well liked by everyone. Other guards that I came in contact with were Ron Smith, Jack Hopkins and Bernard Ware.

In the late spring of 1965 I had just been made up to a slightly higher link and my new regular driver was Ben Ford, a quiet man with a good sense of humour. My first trip with Ben was on the 02.40 down mail to Bournemouth. Bath crews only went as far as Templecombe. Looking at the engine board and seeing it was a 9F I thought it would be quite an easy trip. We backed onto our train; the guard came up to our engine and told us the weight of the train. We had a number of wagons loaded with clay and it was a very heavy load. Ben just looked over at me as if to say, 'well, son, are you up to it?' My next thought was that this was going to be a challenge; we started from Bath with a full head of steam and an almost full boiler. We got between Devonshire and Combe Down Tunnels and I could see that this wasn't going to be as easy as I thought. We were losing steam and the boiler level was dropping and we hadn't got as far as Midford. Of course Ben could see what was happening and did his best to try and help by easing off the gears. We got through the tunnels and Midford and regained some steam and water. Approaching Radstock I felt we were prepared for the eight-mile haul up to the Summit. I had never sweated so much in my life to get where we were. By the time we approached Masbury Summit dawn was beginning to break, our 9F was again in trouble, but I kept at it and on turning over the top I breathed a huge sigh of relief. Of course Ben had looked after me all the way up the climb; he gave me a look of well done, and after this trip we were mates.

It was early September 1965 and it seemed the trains that were running had been reduced in size including almost all passenger services. Even the timetable had been changed to suit the Western Region, but by now everyone knew we were heading for closure. I for one was beginning to get quite dejected with the job; with trains being reduced it meant not so many locos were needed. Many of them were taken out of service and left to rust; some were transferred to other depots en route to the scrap yard. One loco however had not long been transferred to Bath and that was 9F No. 92220 *Evening Star*. I had the pleasure of working on her a number of times. As January 1966 grew closer, the closure date had been extended to early March. My last trip with Ben was on a goods turn but I can't even remember anything about this trip, as I was feeling quite despondent in losing my job, which I loved.

I recall walking down the path leaving railway property for the last time and looking back towards the loco shed with about two or three engines in steam and thinking a year ago there would have been nine or ten. My last thoughts were of the men I had worked with and knew at Bath Green Park, people like Wayne Mayo, Mike Lodder, Alan Larcombe, Dave Boston, Ralph Holden, Archie Gunning, Albert Williams, Dave Massey, Bev Reynolds, Howard Reynolds, Mike Ryall, Norman Gibbons, Dave Williams and Ian Bunnett.

4F No.44560 departing from Bath Green Park with a three-coach set of Bulleid stock. Red and white limited clearance signs are noticeable on the ends of the bridge. (*Martyn Burch*)

In July 1964 4F No.44558 engages in some shunting outside Bath Green Park shed. Another 4F No.44422 (now preserved) is seen in the background. (*Dave Walden*)

7F No.53806 with a freight train for Avonmouth is seen leaving the Midland yard, c.1963. On the right of the photo is Bath station signalbox. (*Martyn Burch*)

9F No.92233 in 1962 with plenty of steam to spare provides a majestic sight as she hauls a train of LMS stock out of Bath Green Park. (*Martyn Burch*)

(*above*) In the summer of 1965, driver Archie Gunning (left) and his fireman Howard Sauqui are about to set off from Bath Green Park with BR Standard class 3MT No.82004. (*Richard Gunning collection*)

(*left*) Driver Ray Stokes in the cab of Templecombe engine 2P No.40634 with his fireman Mike Fudge (right) and shunter Fred Pitman at Bath Green Park. (*Roy Miles*)

(*right*) Bath Green Park Mutual Improvement class plus guests on a day out to Weston-super-Mare in 1953. From left to right, standing, Bob Blake, Sam Stainer, Tom Slip, Tom Gunning, Roy Williams, Archie Gunning, Ken Coffin, Ron Merchant, not known, Dick Evry, Ivor Willshire, Oliver Barnes, Oscar Pitt, Harry Lambert; sitting, Ron Gray?, Sid White, Jack Smith, Jeff Prince, Norman Gibbons, Arthur Selman, George Gray, Doug Holden, Ken Norris, Fred Brooks, Danny Levi, Alan Wilson and George Trevor. (*Roy Williams collection*)

(*above*) Cleaner Arthur Tidball leaning against 4-4-0 No.70's smokebox with fellow male and lady cleaners at Bath loco depot in the early 1900s. Stothert & Pitt's crane manufacturers' building is in the background. (*Desmond Tidball collection*)

Standard class 9F No.92238 with double chimney hauling a Warwick Railway Society Special on 12 June 1965, passing Bellotts Road and soon to cross over the Western main line between Bath and Bristol. I wonder what the man standing on the railings by the roadside could see? Not much with all that steam escaping. (*Martyn Burch*)

Standard class 4 No.75072 having passed through Devonshire Tunnel drifts down under Maple Grove Bridge towards Bath Junction. The first coach appears to be an LMS porthole type. (*Martyn Burch*)

Conditions were really grim in January 1963, as Tony Pitt recalls on the next page. Above, an unidentified Ivatt Tank ploughs its way through the snow and slush out of Green Park. Below, Standard class 5 No.73050 emerges from the southern end of Combe Down Tunnel with a three-coach train. (*both photographs Martyn Burch*)

Tony Pitt

Tony Pitt worked on the S&D for eight years as a fireman at Bath Green Park. His father Ossie worked on the S&D for over 50 years as a driver. Tony has composed this poem of a journey he made with driver Fred Love and guard Fred Nowell. This well-documented incident happened on 3 January 1963, on the 3.30 down goods from Bath Green Park, a near tragic event for the crew (see John Sawyer's memories on page 12).

S&D – 3.30am goods ('63)

Old Fred blew up for the dummy,
The snow was falling fast.
We pulled out of the goods yard
With the banker on our ass.

I slid out the tablet catcher
That protects the single line.
The big eight began to slip a bit,
Fred said: 'Cut that out, you swine'.

We roared up through the Moorfields
With the banker pushing hard,
Racked down at seventy five per cent,
And me losing pounds of lard.

Running free on down to Midford
The tablet I returned.
With a steady run to Radstock
We had a mug of tea well earned.

When steaming through this cold white world,
The blast pipe the only noise,
Was I pleased to be a fireman,
Then the dream of all young boys.

We picked the banker up at Radstock
And headed up for Masbury top.
When the banker left us
We near came to a stop.

The snow was very deep now
And Fred dropped her down the rack.
I had never steamed downhill before,
There would be no going back.

We made it down to Winsor Hill
And she made a sudden stop.
I walked the footplate to the smokebox
Where the snow was near over the top.

Back in the engine on old Fred's side,
Which was a left-hand drive,
The snow was right up to the cab roof,
Enough to bury us alive.

I filled the boiler up with water
And shovelled out all the fire.
To protect the copper firebox
Was the company's main desire.

Another Fred who was our guard
With the pilot to Shepton went.
Lovey and me stayed to protect the train
And in his van our time was spent.

We melted snow to make a brew
On the small stove, which was quite warm.
After some time, we heard a voice calling us –
It was a man from a local farm.

On his tractor, he took us both down
To his home, and his dear wife
Who gave us food and lots of tea,
Which bought us back to life.

Some time after, young Ron Moore turned up
With his permanent way line gang
Who walked us down to Binegar,
And brother, did that take some time.

All were covered in sheets of ice
On faces, boots and clothes.
With phone lines iced nearly two-inch thick,
How we survived, God only knows.

Eighteen hours was the time we spent
Out on the Mendip hills.
Some of us we got away with it,
Knowing conditions like that sometime kills.

In 1964 BR Standard class 4 No.76057 enters Midford with a passenger train bound for Bath. The signalbox can be seen at the end of the platform. Such well-known S&D names as Percy Savage, Harry Wiltshire, Charlie Eyre, Bernard Ware and Laurence Anstice graced this box for many years. (*E.T.Gill/R.K.Blencowe collection*)

The fireman enjoys the view from the cab of Fowler 4F No.44422 as the train heads out of Midford towards Wellow. (*Martyn Burch*)

Standard class 4 2-6-4T No.80138 from Bath with a four-coach train stopping at Wellow, c.1963. Unusually, the locomotive is displaying Southern white discs instead of the usual lamps. The roof of the signalbox can be seen above the second coach. (*C.L.Caddy*)

Wellow station with fresh snow on the ground looks very picturesque. School children are on the down platform with a couple walking gingerly across the icy track. (*Jack Hobbs*)

2P No.40527 and Standard 5 No.73050
passing Wellow with a northbound train for
Sheffield on 23 July 1955. (*R.E.Toop*)

The 13.10 Bournemouth West-Bristol train with Standard class 4 No.76019 in charge, coasts through Shoscombe and Single Hill Halt in May 1963. (*C.L.Caddy*)

7F No.53807 (82F) pilots WC class No.34040 *Crewkerne* near Shoscombe with the 10.38 Manchester-Bournemouth Express on 22 August 1959. (*Keith Barrett collection*)

4F No.44558 and 5MT No.45440 thunder past Writhlington colliery towards Bath, c.1949. The signalbox can just be seen through the haze of the exhaust. (*R.K.Blencowe collection*)

Jinty 3F No.47276 stands next to the Writhlington signalbox after carrying out shunting duties in the nearby colliery sidings. (*SDRT collection*)

Standard class 4 No.75072 piloting 7F No.53810 passes Radstock freight yard going south with a passenger train. The sidings are full with a variety of wagons – open coal, covered vans and engineer vans, possibly of GWR origin. The front coach of the train is a mystery; it seems to have some form of clerestory roof. *(Keith Barrett collection)*

Class 2P No.40564, with fireman John Cockerell, pilots 7F No.53810 through Radstock, having run down the hill from Binegar with an up express. Note that the right-hand window of the signalbox has lost its original curved panes, visible in the photograph on the next page. (*Keith Barrett collection*)

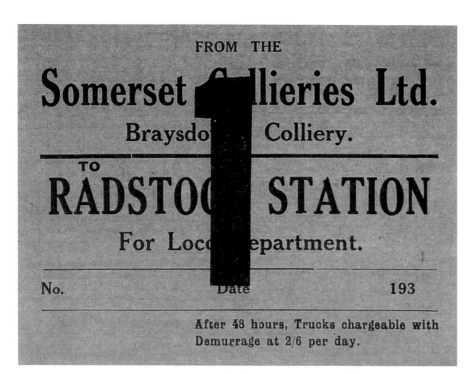

FROM THE

Somerset Collieries Ltd.

Braysdown Colliery.

TO

RADSTOCK STATION

For Loco Department.

No.   Date   193

After 48 hours, Trucks chargeable with Demurrage at 2/6 per day.

(*below*) Radstock station looking towards the Bath to Wells road (A362) level crossing. The down platform with its shelter is empty, whilst the up platform has a barrow with sacks on it, awaiting the next train. The signalbox shows all three windows with the original elegantly curved tops to their panes. Staff who worked here at its zenith were Walt Woods, Dennis Cridland, Phil Crouchen, Steve Jones and Robert Talbot. The memory of Radstock still lives on in the excellent museum in the town. (*Eric Rimmer*)

Standard class 5MT No.73052 passes Radstock North B box with a train for Templecombe on a frosty Christmas Eve in 1963. (*M.W.Knight/Andrew C.Ingram*)

LMS class 2P No.509 and 5MT No.27XX (nicknamed Crab) enter Radstock station after passing over the level crossing in the 1940s with quite a crowd looking on. Note all the vintage cars and vans, worth a fortune today. (*R.K.Blencowe collection*)

(*above*) Driver Fred Hemmings at the controls of a Standard 4 in the 1960s at Midsomer Norton. (*SDRT collection*)

(*left*) Two drivers on the footplate of 8F No.48706 at Norton Hill colliery in 1965. George Tucker, on the left, joined the S&D in 1936 and Horace Clark in 1919. Between them they worked over 70 years on the line. (*George Tucker collection*)

BR Standard class 4 No.75071 with double chimney pulls into Midsomer Norton station with a local passenger train in 1964. (*E.T.Gill/R.K.Blencowe collection*)

Everything is still and quiet at Midsomer Norton except for the permanent way man oiling the point rodding. Theresa Roberts (née Perry), Ken and Larry Dando, Stan Jones, Joe Crouchen, Herbie Cornish and Frank Hamblin all had pride in working here. The S&D Railway Heritage Trust is working hard to restore this station to its former glory. (*Keith Barrett collection*)

(*above*) The signalman leans out of his box as 2P No.40563 enters Midsomer Norton station, c.1959. The platform is busy with schoolchildren waiting to board the train to go home. Hanging baskets and tubs adorn the up platform. (*E.T.Gill/R.K.Blencowe collection*)

(*below*) Viewed from the opposite direction, Standard class 4 No.75071 is seen entering Midsomer Norton with a four-coach train to Bath. Hopefully the injectors would have filled the boiler sufficiently to close the safety valves by the time it arrived at Radstock. The baskets of plants on and around the signalbox and platform give some indication of the splendid display there was in past years. (*Eric Rimmer*)

Jinty class 3F No.47276 is hauling a rake of coal wagons at Midsomer Norton ready to be forwarded to Bath by another loco.
(*Jack Hobbs collection*)

2P No.40563 stops at Chilcompton with a passenger train heading south. Hats off to the staff, the station looks spotless. (*E.T.Gill/R.K.Blencowe collection*)

Porter William Jackson, known to everyone on the S&D as Peter, is holding the family dog Tiny, next to the water tower at Chilcompton station in 1930. The horse was named Kit and Peter's father in-law to be, Fred Golledge, general haulier of Chilcompton, owned the wagon. (*Peter Jackson collection*)

7F No.53808 coasts downhill past the watercress beds at Chilcompton with an up express. Fireman Tony Hicks looks out of his cab as he enjoys a rest. (*Keith Barrett collection*)

01 JUN 1910

SOMERSET & DORSET J. RY. This Ticket is issued subject to the regulations & Conditions stated in the Time Tables & Bills of the Joint Line.

PARLIAMENTARY THIRD CLASS

Bath to

CHILCOMPTON

FARE 1s 2½d   FARE 1s 2½d
CHILCOMPTON   CHILCOMPTON

0118

Standard class 4 No.75073 runs downhill towards Chilcompton Tunnel with a Bath-bound train. The track looks immaculate – Edgar Colbourn, Charlie Burge, Jack Foxall, Walter Gunning and Percy Hill were the unsung heroes of the permanent way. (*Eric Rimmer*)

Fireman Cliff Smith in the cab of a 4F at Binegar station, c.1962. He hasn't changed a bit! (*Cliff Smith collection*)

(*below*) 7F No.53806 hauling a mixed freight destined for Evercreech Junction. At the rear is a 3F Jinty that has banked the train from Radstock up the incline to Masbury Summit. After that, it would then return light engine, wrong road to Binegar and back down to Radstock. (*Eric Rimmer*)

Binegar station after closure. Already weeds are sprouting through the ballast and look at the railings. No more trains would stop here for Bath or to the south. In the good times station staff Fred Uphill, Edgar Smith, Michael Reakes, Norman Down and Frank Staddon were proud to work here. (*Eric Rimmer*)

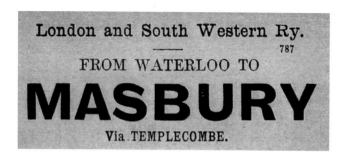

London and South Western Ry.

787

FROM WATERLOO TO

MASBURY

Via TEMPLECOMBE.

(*right above*) This photograph was taken from the road bridge, looking south, as Standard 4 No.76015 climbs through Masbury station towards Binegar. (*Keith Barrett collection*)

(*right below*) BR Standard class 4 2-6-4T No.80134 sweeps past Masbury towards Shepton Mallet with a down local on a bright spring day in 1965. (*C.L.Caddy*)

(*below*) 9F No.92000 is seen at Masbury Summit heading the 09.55 Bournemouth West-Sheffield train in 1961. (*SDRT collection*)

Shepton Mallet station – looking from the south end towards Masbury, with flat-bottom track on the down road, chaired track on the up road. All signals are at danger. On the extreme left can be seen the nearside of a WR Thornycroft lorry. In the car park is a Hillman Minx saloon and up against the railings a Mk.1 Ford Consul. The CWS bacon factory chimney is visible behind the Hillman. Apart from the signalman (his window is open), there is no one about. (*Eric Rimmer*)

LMS 2Ps Nos.323 and 631 double-headed on the up Pines Express entering Shepton Mallet station in 1936. (*SDRT collection*)

A glorious S&D scene as Standard 5 No.73047, having just crossed Charlton Road Viaduct, enters Shepton Mallet with a Bristol-Bournemouth five-coach passenger train. (*Andrew C.Ingram collection*)

Mary Kilmister

My grandmother's house overlooked the S&D Evercreech to Burnham-on-Sea line at Pylle. I spent some of my childhood there, then later with my parents William and Gertrude Webb in a cottage about 100 yards from Shepton Mallet Charlton Road station. At that time I was hardly aware of the S&D, as it would have meant crossing other people's gardens to get to the side of the line.

The only time we went on a train was to visit an aunt and uncle in Bath. I do recall one journey in the war years; we were getting near Bath Green Park station and I could see bombed-out houses. It was a scene of total devastation, with people trying to salvage their possessions. It is a memory I shall never forget. When Bath was bombed one night in April 1942 the bridge over the S&D at Shepton Mallet, which carried the GWR from Witham to Wells, was badly damaged. Our doors and windows were blown in. My mother, five evacuees and myself spent the night in a dugout shelter in the garden. My father was away in the RAF at the time.

My interest in the S&D railway later on made me decide to find a way to the side of the line. One day in 1945 I saw a train pull away from the station going towards Bournemouth packed with wounded soldiers. It was a scene of khaki, bandages, nurses and red crosses, but even with all their problems the soldiers waved to me and smiled.

My friends and I were always told we must never venture onto the railway, but like most kids at that time, empty rails on a Sunday after all the trains had gone were too much of a temptation. We were allowed to wander in the countryside on our own a lot in those days. Nearby there were plenty of small woods and a copse where we picked bluebells, cowslips, celandines and crab apples. Crossing fields that joined the side of the S&D became a natural path for us and we would play on the banks where holes for dugouts had been left from the war, using these as play dens. We were like the Railway Children knowing the times of the trains, the sort of locomotives and, for the most part, who would be on the footplate, not by name of course but by the hats they wore. These were not always railway regulation hats I might add. We also knew that they looked out for us when passing. Many years later I found out some of their names, Ron Gray, Fred Epps, Archie Gunning, Arthur King, Ben Ford, Bill Warren, Bert Reed, Charlie Knight, Dick Windsor and Norman Gibbons.

The porters like William Blacker and Ted Battersby, clerk Emily Poole, guards Frank Staddon, Albert (Dickie) Bird and Bernard Ware, signalman Abe Venner, gangers Fred Moon and Charlie Marshall were all part of our lives, they were always friendly and kind to us. We could not have wished for a better and freer childhood. The S&D always seemed the most important railway, but to get into the station yard at Charlton Road we had to slide down from the GWR bridge over the S&D and into the yard, that way we did not have to cross the lines. We would use the old loading shed in the station as a play theatre, the wooden sleeper platform making an ideal, if rather spongy stage; our audience, real or otherwise, would be down on the lines. We staged great plays here, mostly on a Sunday. We posted a lookout who would climb a small crane in the yard and shout a warning if anyone was coming. One of my friends was Meryl Hanger the stationmaster's daughter; another friend I recall was Molly Banks.

The water pit down by the station was out of bounds, probably because none of us could swim at that time; the viaduct was also a no go area.

On some very cold winter mornings in 1951, the engine crews would bring over a shovel full of fire and put it in the fireplace to boost our own fire. On one of these mornings my father said he thought his future son-in-law would be the fireman that always wore the red beret who my brother always referred to as The Red Hat Man. I thought they were barmy and was most indignant about it all. However, one day on the Bath to Templecombe train the Red Hat fireman came up to me at Bath Green Park station and asked if I would like a trip with the driver, Albert Williams and himself, in the cab. The engine was a class 2P No.40696. In fact I only got in the cab when the train stopped at Binegar; had I not been taken so unaware I would probably have refused. The journey to Shepton was rough to say the least, the footplate rattled and banged. The small wooden seat was much too small and unsteady to sit on. It went at what seemed an incredible speed down over the viaduct into the Charlton Road station. I was more than glad when that piece of ironware came to a standstill. My mother nearly had a fit when I told her that I had a ride on a footplate. After the journey from Bath I would not go through the main exit at the station, but make my way along the railway bank that my father rented as a vegetable garden. So began my S&D railway romance with Bernard; he would come down by train from Bath to see me. Usually he would catch the last train back to Bath when he was on a suitable shift. He would not leave until the train had nearly reached the station, he would then run down the bank across the lines, jump over the five-bar station yard gate and onto the platform catching the train by the skin of his teeth. I rather suspect the footplate crews like Cyril Beale, Ron Shearn, Ron Bean, Fred Epps, Ken Norris and Tom Gunning knew about his courting and would hold up the train for him. In 1956 we got married and the train that took us on honeymoon to Colwyn Bay via Bath Green Park was a Stanier 5 No.45440, assisted by 2P No.40634. We took Bernard's Francis Barnett two-stroke motorbike with us in the guard's van.

When I went to live in Bath I would visit my parents at Shepton Mallet once a week. Catching the train back to Bath Green Park station in the evening, the porter at Bath would help me off with the pram; they were always helpful and friendly. How tragic, when this railway closed; did they really know what they were doing, and how it would affect so many lives?

(*right*) S&D railway clerk Emily Poole enjoys the bright sunshine on the down platform seat of her home station, Shepton Mallet. (*Emily Poole collection*)

(*left*) Driver Pat Evans with an unknown guest on the footplate of an Ivatt class 2 No.41283 at Shepton Mallet. Pat used to take Mutual Improvement classes at Templecombe and helped many a fireman with the rulebook.
(*Stan Blacker collection*)

(*left*) Whilst the young men were away at war the ladies took over some of their roles on the railway, and what a good job they did. Here we see Permanent Way ladies near Evercreech New in the 1940s. Top row, from left to right, May Davies, Mary Tooze and Kath Cable; bottom row, Joan Hughes, Mary Fraser and Rose Ware, with foreman ganger Walter Gunning. Note the porters' hats borrowed from the lads at the station.
(*Rose Ware collection*)

(*below*) Standard class 4MT No.75009 pilots 9F 2-10-0 No.92220 *Evening Star* as it races through Evercreech New and starts the 1:60 climb to the top of the Mendips with this up express.
(*Keith Barrett collection*)

Ken Cook

It is sad to reflect that where I used to work as a porter at Evercreech New station is now a housing estate. The days of a railway community like the S&D have long since gone, but my memories of those days still live on.

My life on the S&D started as a porter at Evercreech New in the early sixties having found out about a vacancy at the New from signalman Pete Ward. Pete was also a part-time butcher. I later found out that a lot of the S&D men had other jobs on the side, from grave digging to selling ice cream from a pushcart. The job was offered to me and I readily accepted the position as a porter. It was long hours for a 16-year-old, as most of the time I worked from 07.00 to 21.30. I had no social life but the rate of pay was incredible, and from day one I was on full porter's wages. There was a variable amount of duties to be carried out, including loading and unloading of goods from local industries, ranging from grain dryers from Gascoigne's to milk powder from Prideaux's. We issued a lot of tickets to school pupils going to Wincanton and Cole. We also had a fair amount of students going to Bath College. Another important duty was the lighting and changing of the signal lamps; you always made sure you paid special attention to the distant signal, as it was a very long walk to it. The lamps always seemed to go out in the winter months when the rain, wind and flurries of snow were at their worst. The 12-plus Tilley lamps on the station were the bane of one's life, having to pump them up and relight them. In the winter your hands froze when trying to light them and you always smelt of paraffin. Other platform tasks were lighting the fires in the waiting room, booking office and the stationmaster's office. You made sure they were topped up with coal throughout the day; otherwise you would be in trouble with the stationmaster if they went out. I recall one incident when Vic Freak was on duty with me, we were attending to a train when a person rushed out of a carriage, and obviously didn't have a ticket. I heard Vic shout out 'Go after him' which I did. I chased him into the fields at the rear of Gascoigne's the engineering company. Fortunately he gave up without any struggle and I hauled him back to the station. In the meantime Vic had phoned the police, and the local policeman, Rhys Davis, who was a very large man, took him away from the station and into custody. I never found out what happened to him.

I always wondered why our stationmaster Reg Jeans used to spend so much time away from the station, but it did not take too long to discover his reason for disappearing; he was in fact in the locality currying favours with companies and individuals to instigate more traffic and revenue for the station. I felt he did a great deal of work in that direction. Reg was a wonderful artist and many of his caricatures can be found in houses even today. Most of the public houses in the area also had Reg's work on display. He was a real stickler for cleanliness and correctness in every way. He always passed comments of some kind on the work. If it wasn't correct you knew it had to be done again. Even his mid-morning cup of tea had to be on time and taken into his office. He would also play cricket with the local children in the nearby field in his lunch hour.

The station had a public footpath through it and many villagers were always resting on the station's seating. Then wonderful conversations developed as I got to know them all. There always seemed to be a lovely smell of food coming from the signalbox when they were about to dine. Signalmen to have dined there include Ted Lambert, Basil Lay, Pete Ward and Norman Rallison.

Late summer evenings after a particularly hot day were very eerie with the track contracting. The wagons seemed to close up making a frightening noise and it took a long time to realize just what it was. On many occasions I armed myself with a brake stick and toured around the station and goods yard anticipating intruders and thieves. I did chase someone one night who was stealing coal but alas I never caught him. One of the permanent way men was a dab hand in netting rabbits along the bank between Evercreech and Shepton Mallet Charlton Road. In the permanent way gang I recall were Alby Knight, Frank Hodges, Ern Giles and Den Poore.

One sad memory I have was the death of railwayman Joe Kemp. It was during the very bad winter of 1962/3 when the snow lay continually for months and conditions for railwaymen to keep the line open were extremely difficult to say the least. Joe set off to walk from his home near Pylle for duty at Evercreech Junction but sadly he didn't make it due to the severe weather conditions. Later that day, somewhere near Elbow Corner, he collapsed and died in the thick snow. I have always found this tragedy quite close to home as I also lived at Pylle; I, too, walked to work that morning and must have passed him on my way to the New. Because of the heavy snow the S&D closed for a short time. When trains started to get through again we were inundated with passengers and goods traffic. The goods had to be stockpiled as all roads were blocked for days and many of our deliveries were down country lanes. When conditions eased off we were busy delivering for weeks. Coal merchants Alan Feaver and Brown Brothers were certainly busy over this period.

As I was the youngest staff member by a lot of years I think I benefited immensely from others; I found everyone chatty and helpful. I think I was the last person to be recruited at Evercreech New before closure in 1966. It was by far the happiest part of my working life and I have fond memories of workmates like driver Bill Rawles, fireman Alan Mason, porters Bill Russell, Vic Freak, Ern Harrop and Ern Hooper, lorry driver Clive Withers and goods checker Charlie Hartnell. I also recall relief stationmaster Wilf Couling who still lives at the station house at Masbury.

(*next page, above left*) With snow on the ground driver Dennis Thorne stands in front of BR Standard 4 No.75072 at Evercreech Junction with a down train. (*Peter Pike*)

(*next page, above right*) Shunter Ken Atkins busy with the shunter's pole at Evercreech Junction as Fred Hicks looks on from the footplate of the Collett. (*Ken Atkins collection*)

(*below*) An early 1900s photo of station staff outside the porters' room at Evercreech Junction. Two of the team in the back row are Ray Atkins and James William Freak, known as Bill. Note the S&DJR fire buckets hanging on the wall. (*Vic Freak collection*)

(*next page, below left*) Bill Freak, c.1919. Bill was a porter and signal lampman for many years on the S&D. Tragically he was killed in a shunting accident at Evercreech Junction on 12 December 1942. (*Vic Freak collection*)

(*next page, below right*) Probably the best known character at Evercreech Junction station was Bill Freak's son Vic – seen here taking a break from bill posting next to the parcels office. (*Vic Freak collection*)

(*above*) Evercreech Junction station viewed from the Templecombe side. On the level crossing weeds shoot up between the rails. The signalbox now empty, the station is deserted. The water tower in the right foreground is redundant. A signal in the background bravely shows danger – but there is no danger; sadly, everyone has gone. (*Eric Rimmer*)

(*left*) Evercreech Junction south signalbox with its 26 levers. This box was home to such signalmen as Arthur Richards, Frank Padfield, Ted Simms and Les Williams. On the left is the *Railway Hotel* where many a railwayman enjoyed a pint after his shift. (*Eric Rimmer*)

A stunning photo of LMS 2P No.698 and Ivatt 4MT No.43012 (nicknamed Doodlebug) heading towards Bournemouth with an express on a gloriously sunny day in 1949. (*R.K.Blencowe collection*)

A horse bus once operated from Station Road, Castle Cary to take passengers to nearby Evercreech Junction station. Note the children enjoying the warm sunshine and posters to such destinations as Swanage, Bournemouth and London. (*SDRT collection*)

Alf Elliott started on the S&D in 1948 as a porter; here he is seen keeping the grass down at Cole. In the background is the station fishpond. Oh for those days again! (*Mick Elliott collection*)

Keeping the permanent way in good order required sheer hard work as can be seen in this early 1900s photo of the Cole gang. Hats were clearly not of a standard issue. (*Keith Barrett collection*)

(*above right*) 13 July 1962 was a sad day for fireman Cliff Smith, seen here on the left with his driver Bill Gunning at Cole on the footplate of 4F No.44560. This was his last but one trip on the S&D before being transferred to Bristol Barrow Road. (*Cliff Smith collection*)

(*below*) Standard class 4 MT No.75071 pulls away from Cole station past the well-known gallows-type signal, over the foot crossing and on to Evercreech Junction. (*Eric Rimmer*)

BR Standard class 3 No.82001 on a down local is about to enter Wincanton station. (*Len Taylor*)

8F No.48706 is seen hauling a down freight train over Verrington Road Bridge (No.132) as two cyclists are about to pass under it. The bridge has now gone except for the abutments. (*Len Taylor*)

The driver is enjoying the Somerset countryside as his BR Standard class 5 No.73052 runs light passing Verrington just north of Wincanton. (*Len Taylor*)

A young trainspotter carrying a camera looks on as BR Standard class 4 No.76026 drifts into Wincanton station with a southbound passenger train. (*Len Taylor*)

On a lovely summer day in the 1960s BR Standard class 5 No.73050 heads a down passenger train through Wincanton. (*Len Taylor*)

Fowler 4F No.44559 leaving Wincanton with a mixed goods train. The rails on the right of the photo served the Cow & Gate milk factory. (*Len Taylor*)

Keith Barrett

At the age of 15 it was time to leave school and I had to find a job with full-time employment, so my grandfather Walt Rogers, who worked in the Carriage & Wagon Department as a wheel tapper at Templecombe, advised me to try to get on the railway at Templecombe depot. I went to the engine shed at Throop Road and saw the shedmaster, Vic Vosper, who asked several questions and gave me an application form to fill in. After a few days, along with Dave Young, I was asked to go for a medical at Swindon. Fortunately I passed and was now ready to start work as an engine cleaner at Templecombe shed.

I started in September 1954 where I was greeted by the clerk Mr Jim Fry (Gentleman Jim we called him) who gave me a rule book which I was to study for future use, particularly rule 55 (the train protection rule). The shedmaster then gave me a tour of the shed and explained the work that lay ahead. So with cloths obtained from the store, it was off to join the rest of the cleaners. Cleaning was a messy job as you had to get into the pit and clean the motion from underneath. The others would be cleaning the rest of the engine before it left the shed. As time passed I was issued with two new pairs of blue bib and brace overalls and one black donkey jacket.

During my time as a cleaner it was also the practice to play jokes on each other. One would be asked to take a bucket of sand to No.2 box as the signalman was having trouble with his wires slipping. Of course the sand was not wanted so by the time you had walked back to the shed your arms felt seven feet long. On the afternoon shift when things were quiet we would all pitch in and have a sloppy fight. This meant oily rags being thrown at each other and us getting in a right old mess. Some of the lads would be right up on the roof of the engine shed waiting to take aim at their next target. On one occasion things got out of hand, Doug Puckett was chasing Mervyn Belbin and on his run Mervyn picked up this bucket half full of oil and turned and threw it all over Doug. That put an end to the sloppy fights for a while.

As a cleaner you were asked to help in all sorts of jobs. These would be filling the coal tubs, emptying the ash pits and getting the fire arch bricks for boilersmith Joe Dyer. Also you would unload stores, light the fire in the sand house, drill out injector clack boxes for the fitters, and rod and steam clean the tubes. During the winter the frost fires at each water column on shed and by the school playground had to be kept going.

We would be asked to join a union, either the NUR or ASLEF, the footplate union. Fireman John Woods collected the dues each week. You got a union magazine for 3d per month. I also got a union badge for 5/6d designed in red, blue, gold and green on a black background, which was stitched onto my blazer top pocket. One night per week I attended a Mutual Improvement class, which was held by driver Pat Evans in the wooden hut high on a bank opposite Templecombe station. This enabled us to understand all about the workings of a locomotive and rules from the rulebook. Pat was a keen instructor and it was a pleasure to attend. On shed during our lunch breaks we would sit in a cabin, which had a big open fire up one end, with a strong wooden table and hard forms for seats. Around the fire there were two big black kettles on the boil and a length of 95lb rail in the shape of a fender. Sometimes we would have to push the table up against the wall to make more room and there would be a challenge between Peter Guy and Derek Howcutt as to who could lift the fender above their head the longest. Another prank we played was after the ashes had been raked out from the ash pan, we would race underneath the engine and urinate on the hot ashes. We would then run out quickly so we didn't get caught, then you looked on to see the fireman in the cab being sick from the smell.

Owing to labour shortages I was made up to a passed cleaner and my venture onto the footplate had begun. First of all I was put on the footplate as second fireman to learn the ropes. The first turn was the 05.05, the 'Early Mail' down train to Bournemouth West with driver Tom Kesteven and fireman Robin Gould. Tom was an organist at Horsington church and was always singing hymns. On arrival at Poole, Tom started cooking his breakfast on the

London and South Western Ry.

787

TO

TEMPLECOMBE

shovel – eggs, bacon and two sausages. This was short-lived as Robin accidentally hit the blower and his two rashers disappeared into the fire grate; Tom went mad. On another turn I had to start at 03.35 along with driver Ben Dyer and Mervyn Belbin on the 04.20 freight to Evercreech Junction. On approaching Wincanton, Merv and I were leaning out of the cab having a chat when he decided to put on a few more shovels of coal. To our amazement, on turning around, we found our driver was missing from the footplate. Ben was outside on the running board looking back through the driver's window, just like a ghost. Arriving at Evercreech up sidings we would all go into the shunter's cabin for a break. Head shunter George Green was on the phone to Bath control, in walked Merv with his guitar and started to play a few tunes. This didn't go down too well with George and he quickly kicked Mervyn out and locked the door.

Soon after I was allowed to go out onto the footplate as a fireman. I required a hand brush to keep the footplate clean and a billycan for a brew up. We were sent to many different places to work, as other depots were short of firemen. I went to Salisbury station, Southampton docks, shunting at Poole and on loan to Branksome, Evercreech Junction, Highbridge and Bath. On one occasion I had to go to Bath, spare on the cushions, and was booked along with driver Dick Evry to work to Gloucester and back. On the outward journey we had a Midland 'Crab' and on the return it was a Standard class 5.

Another memory was on the night shift in No.3 link, with driver Charlie Gould on the top end shunter. The engine was a G6 0-6-0 No.30274. It was so busy you would be going backwards and forwards all shift. During this time 8,000 wagons a week would leave the yard. You had to keep watch during these movements otherwise you would have your head knocked off as the wagons were so close to the next siding. In foggy weather the head shunter would operate the yard light switch for you. He did this, as you were unable to see his hand signal and would not know what movement he required. One Thursday I was booked on to take a light engine to Bath for repair at Derby with driver Ron Spiller. We had to travel home spare afterwards on the 09.03 ex Bristol T.M. This particular Thursday was a Wincanton race day and Prince Monolulu was travelling on our train in his full

regalia. What an excellent sight that turned out to be. Leaving Wincanton I found that one of the passengers who had just left the train, had left his wallet behind. It was full of money and belonged to a gentleman from Bristol, so I gave it to Ron, who then handed it to acting shedmaster Harry Jeans to investigate.

One Saturday I was on the night return, working the 22.00 up passenger with driver Ken Perry on a Standard class 5 No.73054 and running the fire down at Sturminster Newton. On approaching Stalbridge distant signal Ken started to apply the brakes and we gradually came to a halt by the home signal. On opening the fire hole doors I found there was not enough steam to draw the brakes off; the fire was almost out. Panic set in, more coal was put on the fire and 27 minutes later we moved off at a slow pace. Arriving late at Templecombe Upper station the guard handed Ken a lost time ticket so some explaining had to be done.

After assisting a train to Bath with driver Gordon Hatcher we had our lunch and then took a visit to Thos. Best shop just off Milk Street where I bought a billhook for 2/6d thinking it was the best around, but little did I know that Thos was short for Thomas. We've had a good laugh about it ever since, and I'm still using the hook.

Another trip involved driver Ken Nutland and fireman Ernie West. They had to bring Standard class 5 No.73050 back to Temple-combe shed, working light engine from Branksome. Approaching Stourpaine Bridge Ken shut the regulator without putting the blower on; the back-draft blew the flames out into the cab, burning Ernie's new overall to shreds all down the outside of the left leg.

When Steve Collins transferred as a driver to Templecombe shed from Yeovil Town I was booked to work with him on the 18.05 (Sat) Templecombe-Bournemouth West train. He found out that we had WC class No.34041 *Wilton* on this trip. So he asked driver Harry Saunders what these engines were like running on the 'Dorset'. He told him to keep them running through Corfe Mullen Junction to get up the bank. Of course as Steve was a Southern engineman it was just what he wanted to hear. Off we went, but as *Wilton* was a bad steamer we were struggling for steam and water all the way, but somehow coped. Approaching Corfe Mullen with a clear road we collected the tablet and went through the crossover like hell. With me wearing hobnail boots and trying to rescue the tablet, I couldn't stand on my feet; I thought we were coming off the road. I became so frightened that I had to sit down, as I was shaking with fear until Broadstone was in sight. Further on as we swept through Creekmoor Halt we crossed the siding points at speed. He then had me in another panic as the engine wobbled side to side. By the time we had arrived at Bournemouth West we were in a poor state of affairs. Before we could move again, I had to work up some steam to get the water back into the boiler before we could reverse our stock back up into the carriage sidings. It sure was a journey that I have never forgotten.

call the signalman at No.2 box and ask permission to leave the shed, as it was only a single line. On walking to the phone it was raining very hard. I phoned No.2 box and the signalman Harry Bowles answered; I asked him: 'Is it okay to leave the shed?' Just then an almighty clap of thunder sounded overhead and a great flash of lightning lit everything up as it struck the wires. Before I could speak to him again I was thrown backwards and hit the ground unable to move. Dick ran to me right away and got some help to carry me into the cabin. There I stayed as I was unable to stand on my legs and another cleaner was booked to go along with Dick whilst I was taken home.

Ex-SR class G6 No.30274 arrives on Templecombe shed on 16 July 1955. Keith Barrett steps down from the footplate to get the engine coaled by means of the hoist and tubs seen on the right of the picture, in readiness for its next turn, as top end shunter. (*Keith Barrett collection*)

I recall one day I was with driver Dick Rendle; our loco was 7F No.53802 and we were on the 17.45 freight to Evercreech Junction. It was the fireman's duty to go to the phone, which was fixed in a box and hung on the far end of the engine shed wall. You always had to

After working with the drivers in No.2 Link and with the spare drivers as required, it was time for me to move into No.1 Link (passenger) as a fireman on a regular basis. My driver now was Den Norris who was a member of the Magic Circle and a Justice of the Peace at Wincanton Court. He was a good driver who would do everything according to the book. After assisting the Pines Express we had a break to visit the shops. We went to Woolworth's and found the toy section. He wanted to purchase some items to use in his act as a magician. He got me to look through a six-inch long black tube, which you turned to see the coloured lights. I couldn't see anything, so he suggested I try the other eye. Still not seeing anything, he placed it back on the shelf and left. When we got back to the shed several workmates were grinning from ear to ear. It was only when I got home and looked in the mirror I could see the reason why. I had one big black ring around each eye, which was caused by the black felt ends of the tube.

Things soon began to change again as Den was having difficulty attending the court sessions, so he arranged to change jobs with Ray Stokes permanently. I was to become fireman to driver Ray Stokes. This move was to start another chapter in my railway career. It became apparent that Ray would work an engine more heavily and always liked to make up time, so steam was not to be in short supply. Ray always carried a black tin box with a brass plate on the lid with his name proudly engraved. As we got to know each other we discovered that we both liked a game of crib, so I always carried a crib board and a pack of cards ready to play a game whenever a spare moment became available. In this link we only had 12 shifts, which were worked over a three-month cycle. We soon had a good relationship and would help each other out whenever we could. Having worked the 22.25 last down passenger from Bath to Templecombe we berthed the stock in the neck and were ready to run the engine to shed but we were stopped by the station signalbox on the dummy. The signalman Eric Knight opened his window and shouted out: 'You've got no lights lit'. I shouted back :'Have you got any matches?' When he replied 'Yes', I answered: 'You had better come and light them'. He was so mad he slammed his window shut and all the glass fell out. The dummy was pulled off to green and a quick departure to the shed was made. We were never told to light the lamps again after that.

After a while Ray had a word with me and he allowed me to do some driving whilst he took the turn as fireman. It didn't matter what shift we were working, I would be doing the driving on the outward journey,

every Tuesday and Thursday, and on the homeward journey on Wednesday and Friday. I was very proud to do this and it was very kind of Ray in allowing me to take on such a responsibility.

I was driving the 08.55 up passenger with Standard class 5 No.73054, and on leaving Bailey Gate I noticed the hounds were running across the track ahead. As I drew near to Sturminster Marshall Bridge I applied the brakes and stopped. The huntmaster (Portman hunt) called the hounds clear and waved to us to re-start our train. The next day Ray came to me on shed as I was disposing of an engine and gave me £10, explaining that the hunt had sent us £20 for stopping and not killing any of their animals. So he agreed to split the money evenly between us.

Two engines that I shall always remember were class 2P No.40634, the engine regularly used as assistant for the Pines Express, and Standard class 4 No.75027, which always worked the 11.40 up passenger train.

In 1961 the last class 2P was used as a pilot engine and was replaced by Standard class 4MT 4-6-0s. Then the 9Fs started to arrive for use at Bath, and the last Pines Express ran over the 'Dorset' on 8 September 1962, then transferred to another route.

During early 1963 I was driving home the 14.20 from Highbridge when we stopped in deep snowdrifts near the top of Pylle bank. Ray got permission from our guard Reg Brewer to reverse back down to Pylle station to try again. He took over the controls and off we set with the engine in full forward gear and second regulator. We hit the drifts, the engine jumped upwards with the snow disappearing over the top of the cab roof. I honestly thought we were off the road, but fortunately we weren't. Ray got us safely into Evercreech Junction station and I drove on towards Templecombe.

With the job looking a bit shaky I left the railway on 28 January 1964. On my very last day I walked into the lobby to find Ray and Den Norris filling in their driver's ticket. I shook hands and said goodbye to them both. I left Templecombe shed for the last time, a very sad occasion for me.

I remember my driver Ray Stokes with pride for being such a brilliant workmate. Also, all the other staff at Templecombe shed and everywhere along the 'Dorset', they all were good friends. It's a great pity that it had to end.

Shed staff Charlie Guy (*left*) and Walt Webb stand in front of a very clean BR Standard 5 No.73050 (now preserved) on Templecombe shed. (*Trevor Jeans collection*)

(*left*) Guard Ted Scovell at Templecombe on the last night of service on 5 March 1966. (*Rodney Scovell*)

Driver Pat Evans (*left*) and fireman Mike Baker on the footplate of Ivatt class 2MT No.41290 with the 12.05 Templecombe-Bath train in December 1965. (*Mike Baker collection*)

(*right*) Fitter Ken Arnott is busy making spring clips in the fitters' work-shop at Templecombe shed in 1958. (*Rodney Scovell*)

(*below*) The darts and skittle team from the *Royal Hotel*, Templecombe in the 1950s:
(*back row, from left to right*) Maurice Miles, Jack Hix, Fred Gray, Percy Hobbs, Den Morgan, Harry Jeans; (*middle row*) Vic Brixey, Ray Darke, Gordon Hatcher, Norman Light, Jack Rendle, Den Norris; (*front row*) Charlie Hawkins, Clarence Thomas, Mrs. Dukes (the landlady), Art Hatcher, Jim Hatchley, John Dray. (*Gordon Hatcher collection*)

Driver Bill Miles leaning against the buffer and fireman Robin Gould with 2P No.40569, c.1961. She was withdrawn a short time after this photo was taken. (*Peter Pike*)

In May 1961 at Templecombe Lower, Ern Cawley stands in front of class 3 2-6-2T No.40171. Note the recent damage to the left buffer. (*Peter Pike*)

Signalman Bob Drew in Templecombe No.2 box in October 1963. How clean and tidy it looks. (*Peter Pike*)

Templecombe railwaymen in the 1950s. From left to right, Bert Davis, Ron Mortimer, Bert Everett, Frank Styling, Ron Fudge and shunter Reg Day. (*Gordon Hatcher collection*)

The most important ladies on the S&D – they looked after the refreshment room on Templecombe station. From left to right, Joan Miles, Winnie Hannam and Dolly Sanger. (*Roy Miles*)

Guards Roy Miles and Reg Brewer enjoy a box of chocolates, given to Reg by a grateful passenger on the last day of service in March 1966. Note Roy's S&D footwear. (*Roy Miles collection*)

The Pines Express on 6 July 1938, with LMS class 5MT No.5194 in charge, has just passed No.2 box at Templecombe heading south for Bournemouth. (*H.C.Casserley*)

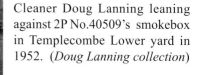

Cleaner Doug Lanning leaning against 2P No.40509's smokebox in Templecombe Lower yard in 1952. (*Doug Lanning collection*)

0-6-0 Scottie No.40, built at Vulcan foundry in 1879 and withdrawn in 1930, is on the turntable at Templecombe on 12 June 1926. One of the crew appears to be oiling the motion. (*H.C.Casserley*)

Coaling Ivatt 2MT No.41248 on Templecombe shed with, from left to right, Walt Webb (steamraiser, tipping) Ern Cawley (coalman, driving the electric crane) and Vic Lephard (labourer). (*Keith Barrett collection*)

Mutual Improvement Class lads of Templecombe depot on an outing in the 1950s. Standing from left to right, Len Hardee, Ray Stokes, Fred Gray (in the coach), Reg Burt, Ray Darke, Ken Day, Syd Boussey, John Dray and Fred Fisher; front row, Norman Light, Percy Hobbs, Wilf Jeans. (*Fred Fisher collection*)

Bernard Curtis

My days on the S&D started in 1947. I worked at Templecombe motive power depot as a passed cleaner. Workmates there at the time included Len Counsell, Joe Dyer, Fred Chant, Chris Amesbury, Ted Elliott, Cecil Cooper, Rodney Scovell, Jack Osborne and Charlie Watkins. In between the hard work on the footplate there were some lighter moments, as very often passed cleaners from Templecombe were sent out to Evercreech Junction to take over from one of the firemen on the Junction's shunting engine. One particular day I was out there on the afternoon shift along with driver Chris Amesbury. At about 15.00 it was the custom to send the shunting engine down to the Junction's goods shed and bring back a couple of box vans which had been loaded down there. The signalman at the north box directed us out onto the main line that led to the station and as we approached the home signal; it was at danger, so of course we stopped. Although Chris blew the whistle several times the signal remained on. We could see no movement of anyone in the box so after a few minutes Chris said to me, 'You had better go down and see what the problem is'. I walked down the track and along the platform and as I was passing the toilets I heard loud shouting coming from the gent's side. It turned out that the signalman Tom Ashman had gone in to the gent's when there was no traffic about. Unfortunately for him the lock, which was rather ancient, had jammed and he was trapped inside. The platform staff had gone to their messroom for afternoon tea and of course did not hear his shouts. I alerted one of the station staff and he was released looking rather embarrassed.

One day, I was on the early morning Hamworthy goods train with driver Percy Hobbs. We used to book on about 02.30 for this turn, go light engine to Evercreech Junction and then take the train to Hamworthy Junction and return light engine to Templecombe. When we ran into Blandford Forum on our return trip we always had to wait for anything up to ten minutes for the 09.10 passenger train from Templecombe to clear the line from Shillingstone. On this particular day Percy decided we had time for him to have his hair cut at the barbershop just outside the station. 'When we have to go, just touch the whistle', he said, but unfortunately for Percy the passenger train came in earlier than usual. After it had

departed the signalman pulled off our signal and came round and gave me the single line tablet; we were now right of way. I touched the whistle and Percy came running up and jumped on the footplate. He opened up the regulator and we were away. I shouted across to him and asked if he had managed to have his haircut; Percy replied with a grin: 'Well, the barber's done one side and if I return tomorrow he will do the other side'.

In 1953 I failed a colour vision test to become a registered fireman. I was then transferred to the fitting shop at Templecombe loco depot and given the job of fitter's mate to Bert Hughes. Other fitters and mates there at that time were Frank Iley, Ken Arnott, Arthur Elliott and Bert Rolls. We were employed on all the regular maintenance jobs and running repairs, as they occurred, to all the locomotives.

One incident I recall quite vividly happened in 1958. Bert and I were on the night shift and were always liable to be called out on any derailments in our area; usually it was a minor derailment like an engine or a goods wagon becoming derailed on points whilst shunting. We had a breakdown van made out of a converted luggage van, equipped with tools, steel plates and wood packing for getting the wheels back on the track. There was also a stove we could light up and brew some tea on when out on a long job. At that time the last train at night down from the Highbridge branch was a goods, always known as the Highbridge Market. From West Pennard station to Evercreech Junction the route involved climbing quite a steep incline for several miles. On the night of this incident the weather was very damp and no doubt the line was quite greasy. The train was made up of quite a few goods vans loaded with tinned milk, all packed in cardboard boxes, which was part of a consignment for shipping to Malta. As the train neared the top of the incline the engine slipped violently on the greasy rails, which caused the coupling behind the engine to snap. The whole train went running back down the incline towards West Pennard. The crossing keeper at Stean Bow saw the train running back and phoned the signalman at West Pennard to inform him. He thought the train was setting back because it could not make it up the incline. He turned the points for the siding; the train then hit the buffer blocks at the end of the siding and all the goods vans piled up on top of one another. Luckily the guard's van did not collapse and the guard, Ted Scovell, was not too badly injured but he was in a state of shock, which was to be expected.

Our breakdown gang was ordered to go to the scene of the accident as soon as possible. An engine was obtained to take us there in our breakdown van. When we arrived, some time after midnight, the scene that greeted us, from what we could see with our limited lighting, was one of utter chaos. Goods vans were piled high across the track and, in the nearby field, doors were ripped open with boxes of tinned milk lying everywhere. It was beyond us to try and clear the line. A heavy lifting crane was required and the nearest was some distance away, in Salisbury. We spent the rest of the night off-loading the tinned milk from the wreckage, which of course would make them lighter for the crane to lift when it arrived. I had never known such a long night. When daybreak arrived everyone was hungry so I went along the road to a wayside shop and obtained some bread, butter and eggs. We boiled the eggs in a tea can, two at a time, and with a new clean blade in the hacksaw sliced up the bread (no sliced bread in those days) and of course we had milk all around us for our brew. The crane eventually arrived and began lifting the goods vans from the running lines. It was well into the afternoon before the line was cleared.

We arrived back in Templecombe late in the afternoon. My mate insisted that we came back to do our normal night-shift that night otherwise we would lose a night's pay and what overtime we had done would not do us much good. This we did but only the really essential jobs were done. After this we had several Sundays working at West Pennard clearing up the remaining trucks in the field. Bert always liked using the acetylene cutters and he certainly enjoyed himself down there. We also had a good stock of tinned milk for ages.

Fitter's mates Bernard Curtis (*left*) and Arthur Elliott in front of an Ivatt class 2 at Templecombe Lower yard in 1956. (*Bernard Curtis collection*)

Down view of Henstridge station in the 1960s. This was the smallest station on the line, the platform being only 150 feet long. The last person to work here was the well-liked Albert (Dickie) Bird. (*Eric Rimmer*)

Driver Bert Jones on the left and fireman Raymond Coates leaving Henstridge station with a full head of steam on 9F No.92220 *Evening Star*. (*Robin Gould*)

Porter David Hughes enjoying a rest in the summer of 1963 after coming off duty from Henstridge station, which can be seen in the background.
(*David Hughes collection*)

The Jeans Family

Frederick Harry Jeans joined the S&D as a porter at Stalbridge in the very early 1900s. Frederick, a hard working and dedicated S&D man, was seldom seen on the platform without a tie or rose in his lapel.

His son Walt followed in his footsteps in the early 1920s. He went onto the footplate and became a senior driver at Templecombe. Walt gave over 50 years' service to the railway, mostly on the S&D. He was a fine engineman who was respected by all the colleagues who worked with him.

The natural thing for Walt's son Trevor to do was to follow his grandfather, father, uncles and cousins onto the railway. In 1956 he started as a junior porter at Templecombe, then in 1960 he became a signalman at Corfe Mullen. At 19 he was one of the youngest signalmen on the S&D at the time. Unfortunately for Trevor and many more families the S&D closed in March 1966. Happily, memories live on and, by courtesy of Trevor, a selection of the family's photographs are featured on these two pages.

(*top left*) 18-year-old Frederick Harry Jeans stands proudly in his railway uniform complete with a rose in his buttonhole. Note the Somerset Joint Committee badge on his lapel.

(*top centre*) Frederick, now a senior porter at Stalbridge, has his photo taken in 1930. Again a lovely rose is prominent and note his bushy hair.

(*top right*) An early photo of Walt taken at Templecombe in 1930.

(*left*) BR Standard class 4 No.76012 with Walt on the left and his fireman Ray Howcutt at Wincanton.

(*above*) A splendid shot of Walt with his hand
on the regulator of a Collett class loco.

(*right*) Trevor gazes out from his signalbox
at Corfe Mullen. This box opened in 1905
and had 24 levers. It controlled the Junction
and the double section from Bailey Gate, as
well as the single line to Broadstone.

(*above*) Stalbridge station on 6 August 1965 with Ivatt 2MT No.41283 on the 12.30 Templecombe to Branksome and Standard 4MT No.76057 on the 11.40 Bournemouth Central to Bristol train just entering the station. (*Tim Chapman*)

(*left*) Guard Phil Hatcher, looking very smart, raises the green flag to his driver at Stalbridge station in the 1950s. (*Phil Hatcher collection*)

LMS Black 5MT No. 5440 sprints through the Dorset countryside with a mixed train near Stalbridge on 7 July 1938. (*H.C.Casserley*)

Class 2P No.40601 drifts past Hammoon towards Sturminster Newton with a down stopper. (*Keith Barrett collection*)

Standard class 4MT No. 75073 with a full head of steam passes Hammoon overbridge with an up passenger train. (*Keith Barrett collection*)

A superb panoramic view of Sturminster Newton signalbox, station and yard. Note the Ford Thames van on the right next to some box wagons. (*Trevor Jeans collection*)

Station staff at Sturminster Newton in 1930; back row, from left to right: Bill Vincent, (Happy) Clark, Bill Stacks, Joe Marsh, Walt Fudge, Mr. Moore; front row: Arthur Pope, Percy Lydford, Elsie Clarke, Bill Lush, Henry Upshall, Jack Inkpen. (*Elsie Drew collection*)

Gerald Trowbridge

Gerald started at Sturminster Newton station as a junior porter in March 1944. His father Frank was also a porter there for over 20 years. There were a few characters at the station, one of them an old porter, Walt Fudge, nicknamed 'Sticker', who was 6ft 3ins tall. When passenger trains came in, Walt was always first in line to get the tips.

Gerald was at the station for two years, when he got the footplate bug. He was invited to ride in the cab of a class 3F Bulldog by driver Den Norris. After that he transferred to Templecombe motive power depot as a cleaner. He enjoyed getting to know all about the different engines. Part of the job was to empty the ash pits, and then coal the engines on an old-fashioned coal stage, which was hard work as the coal tubs were wound up by hand. He then progressed to a passed cleaner. His first firing turn was on a passenger train with driver 'Doctor' Montague, so-called because of the doctor's bag he carried with him. They were on a Black 5 No.5056, his first time on that class of engine, and he thought his dreams had come true. Gerald had worked mostly on 2Ps, so to climb aboard and see the spacious cab with its look of sheer power was quite daunting for a young lad. The footplate floor was clean and the controls were shining, he felt he was firing on a Rolls Royce.

Another driver he worked with was George Williams; he liked his breakfast of bacon and eggs cooked on the shovel. Gerald used to warm a pork pie on the clack box, and with a can of tea it was a good start to the day.

One memorable journey was on a 3F, running light on a banking duty. The driver, Fritz Lawrence, stopped in a cutting where there were lots of rabbits running around. He pulled out the 12-bore shotgun which he had leaning up against the reversing lever and started popping away at these rabbits. Fritz said to Gerald: 'When they fall down you get off the footplate and go and pick them up'. He was not a very good shot and Gerald didn't have to get off the footplate too much. There was never a dull moment with him, he enjoyed his scrumpy and always carried a quart bottle with him. He was also a part-time bookmaker, taking bets on the horses for everybody. He certainly introduced Gerald to life and was always very helpful to him. One of the rostered turns was to work the 'Mail train' from Templecombe Lower to Bournemouth and work the 'Pines Express' back with the oil-burning engines. They were not very successful at the time, but much easier than using a shovel.

He was called up for National Service where he served 23 months in the Royal Engineers. He was hoping to get on the railway, but no such luck, he spent most of the time bridge building. He returned to the railway and now made the big time as a registered fireman with regular turns, working with driver and good friend Bert Jones. They worked together for eight months, and then he moved to the passenger link, firing to one of the most famous drivers on the railway, Art Hatcher. Working with these various characters, there was many a tale to be heard. Gerald recalls a story told by guard Frank Staddon. A footplate crew were travelling on a 7F, pulling a freight train. The fireman saw a goat on the line and told his driver to stop. The fireman got off the cab and caught the goat; they decided to put him in the cab and take him to the next station, as they were in the middle of nowhere and he was certainly lost. Now the fireman, being a bit of a joker, decided to play a game on signalman Sid Pitt. They were passing his signalbox before they got to the next station. The fireman put his jacket and hat on the goat; as they approached the signalbox he lifted his two front legs up and put them on the side of the cab facing the box. The fireman ducked down as they went past; Sid's face was a picture. He phoned his mate in the next signalbox and said, 'This freight train has just come through, I don't know who that fireman was, but he has got a face just like a goat'.

Another story involved his shedmaster Bernard Dyer, who always wore a bowler hat and called everybody 'Mee Sonny'. A certain passed cleaner was late for his turn. When Mr. Dyer asked him why, the passed cleaner gave him some backchat. Mr. Dyer was not impressed and, moving his bowler hat to the back of his head, said 'Now look here, mee sonny, you go home and when you pass the Co-op, go in and buy yourself a bar of carbolic soap. Then go home and wash your mouth out, stay home tomorrow and give it a good rinse out. You come back the next day and I will decide whether I will start you'.

Gerald was well liked and enjoyed the close comradeship of mates like Fred Fisher, Walt Jeans, Charlie Watkins and Bert Jones. His wife Lilian lived near the line at Stalbridge when they were courting. When Gerald passed through on his engine, he would give her a special little whistle. If it happened to be in the evening she would lean out of the upstairs window, waiting to hear her secret message.

Class 4F No.44417 (82G) prepares to leave Sturminster Newton after shunting off some cattle trucks. There is much discussion going on among the staff at the line side. (*M.W.Knight/Andrew C.Ingram*)

Somerset & Dorset Railway Trust engine 7F No.53808 passes Shillingstone signalbox with the LCGB Somerset & Dorset Rail Tour on 30 September 1962. (*Keith Barrett collection*)

Shillingstone station just after closure in 1966. It had been a working station for 103 years. Perhaps the buildings can be saved as a permanent reminder of a Dorset country station where loyal staff Bob Downes, Harry Guy, Percy Ladd, Edward Rhymes, Harold Hooper and many others worked. (*Tim Chapman*)

Stourpaine & Durweston Halt had a small shelter and an SR-style concrete platform. It opened in 1928 and closed 28 years later. (*C.L.Caddy*)

Standard 4MT No.76062 at Blandford with a stopping train to Bournemouth West. Note the high-sided 'BR1B' tender coupled to this loco.
(*Keith Barrett collection*)

Standard class 4 No.76015 (71A Eastleigh) stands at Blandford Forum with a morning train to Bournemouth. The station looks busy with passengers and freight. (*M.W.Knight/ Andrew C.Ingram*)

(*left*) An unidentified class 5 loco, with shed code 82F (Bath Green Park), southbound at Blandford Forum in July 1964. A number of box wagons stand in the siding and what look like bags of fertilizer on a lorry belonging to Blandford & Webb. This scene depicts a busy station, where over the years, staff like Arthur Bowen, Fred Dennis, Vic Beale and Walt Holly looked after the passengers and goods traffic.
(*Dave Walden*)

S&D 4-4-0 No.70, built at Derby in 1914, later to become No.39 in 1928. The loco is seen at Blandford Forum, waiting to leave with a passenger train. Note the fireman tiptoeing across the tender. (*Jack Hobbs collection*)

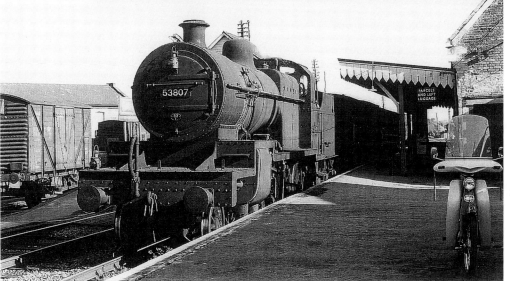

Class 7F No.53807 (82F) stops at Blandford Forum with the 15.05 freight Poole yard-Templecombe Upper on 28 August 1964. Note the Honda 50 moped in the foreground. (*Keith Barrett collection*)

WC class No.34102 *Lapford* leaves Blandford with a down schools excursion in 1964. (*Keith Barrett collection*)

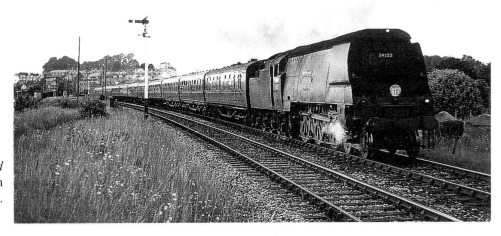

The station staff at Blandford Forum in 1923: back row, from left to right, Joe Penny, Maurice (Sam) Simms, Herbert Wort, Fred Hazzard, Ern Stickley, Frank Marshall, Walt Warren; middle row, Joe Luff, Reg Sharlon, Alfred Dowdney, Henry (Ewart) Gulliford; front row, Vic Beale, Arthur (Giant) Pope, Fred Dennis. (*Mike Beale collection*)

Harold (Nobby) Whiting, on the right, receiving a presentation from British Railways after 36 years service. Nobby spent most of his railway life on the S&D. He enjoyed many years at his home station of Blandford Forum as the senior porter.
(*Maud Whiting collection*)

WC class 4-6-2 No.34105 Swanage (now preserved) passes Charlton Marshall with a down express in August 1959.
(*Keith Barrett collection*)

In the early 1900s lengthmen at Spetisbury are busy working on the up track. The building alongside the base of the starting signal is the signalbox.
(*Keith Barrett collection*)

Another turn-of-the-century view of Spetisbury station, looking north. Note the old spelling of 'Spettisbury'. The station opened in 1860 and closed to passengers in 1956. The official on the right appears to be the stationmaster.
(*Keith Barrett collection*)

A fine shot of Fowler 4F No.44557 with a goods train about to leave Bailey Gate station. The fireman is busy on top of the tender. Note the milk tanks on the right at the United Dairies factory, formerly Carter's & Dorset Modern Dairies. *(R.C.Riley)*

Station staff at Bailey Gate, taken in 1927. From left to right, standing, stationmaster Edmond Ham, booking clerk Neil Clarke, shunter Harry Scovell; sitting down, porters George Dennis, George Biles and Percy Carter. (*Bill Coomer collection*)

Fred Andrews leans over the veranda of Bailey Gate crossing signalbox, next to the A31, as BR Standard 4MT No.75073 drifts past with a short passenger train in 1963. (*C.L.Caddy*)

The signalman at Corfe Mullen Junction hands the tablet to the fireman of class 4 No.76026 on the 06.00 Bristol to Branksome train on 3 August 1965. (*Tim Chapman*)

7F No.53807, built at Derby in 1925, hauls eight coaches past Broadstone signalbox in 1962. She was withdrawn from service in October 1964. (*C.L.Caddy*)

Standard class 4MT No.80146 draws into Creekmoor Halt. The platform looks full, as the passengers head for Poole or Bournemouth. How the women with their prams must have missed the station when it closed. (*C.L.Caddy*)

Tim Chapman

My interest in the S&D originates from having a father who was brought up in Poole but who married and settled in Manchester. Through the fifties, this meant taking the Pines Express in my formative years to stay with my grandparents and aunt who were still living near to Poole station. Despite moving to Darlington in 1959 I still managed journeys over the S&D and in particular a journey back to Manchester to see a former school friend. This was on 1 September 1962 and I realised that it could well be the last trip I would make on a through train to the north via Bath. For many years I had been one of the army of trainspotters armed with the Ian Allan listings of the steam locomotives of those times. The S&D showed me that there was much more to a railway than engine numbers, and that wider interest

in the line as a whole lasted not only to the end of the line but to the present day.

Visits to our relatives in Poole provided ideal opportunities to travel on the line and I had the privilege of travelling on over 40 S&D trains during these holiday weeks. With the Pines having been re-routed, the best train of the day from the Poole area up the S&D had been lost. The next best was the 11.40 semi-fast from Bournemouth which left Poole at 11.49 and arrived in Bath at 13.53. Excursion fares were available on this train, 11/3d for a day excursion to Bath, if my memory serves me well. This allowed return travel by any train, of which the most obvious was the 16.20 semi-fast from Bath, but only gave two hours to explore the historic city and the engine sheds! The other return through train was the 19.05 from Bath, which would get me back to Poole just after 22.00. There were other possibilities made available using the other stopping trains. The first was the 15.20 from Bath. I caught this as far as Midsomer Norton or Binegar to photograph the 16.20 from Bath coming up the 1 in 50 Mendip gradients before catching the 16.35 stopper from Bath from each of these stations. The 15.20 and the 16.20 also connected with branch trains from Evercreech Junction at 17.00 and 18.02 to Highbridge. The latter was a bit more risky, it involved a sprint over the footbridge at Highbridge to catch the 19.10 back to Evercreech, which would be waiting to leave. Failure to catch this would mean being stuck overnight!

Perhaps the most dramatic journey I made up the S&D was on 28 December 1964, my 17th birthday and just over a year before closure, though of course we didn't know that at the time. My family had all decided to come with me that day up to Bath from Poole. As dawn broke, crisp frosty sunshine reflected off a good coating of snow. Was this a good day to go to Bath? How much snow would there be on the Mendips? How late would trains be running? With the 11.40 from Bournemouth still some time off, I went down to Holes Bay Junction to see the earlier S&D trains, the 07.35 from Templecombe and the 09.40 from Bournemouth. The former train provided the engine for our run up to Bath, so our prospects looked bleak when it arrived all of 96 minutes late on a journey that should have only taken 73 minutes. The latter train, however, was only six minutes late from Poole.

We decided to chance it and things looked good when our Standard class 4 engine No. 75072 left Bournemouth West just 19 minutes late. Southbound trains were still not doing so well though. The 05.58 from Bristol (06.48 from Bath) should have reached Bournemouth West at 10.47 but in fact struggled in at 11.55 just before our train left. The first S&D train we saw en route was one that the 11.40 would normally not pass at all, the 06.35 freight from Evercreech Junction. We passed it at Bailey Gate running some two hours later than usual and comprised of two guards vans, but no revenue-earning wagons.

The next passing sequences, however, happened as normal. The 09.03 semi-fast from Bristol (09.53 from Bath) passed us at Blandford a mere 20 minutes late, and the 12.23 stopper from Templecombe was waiting

for us at Stalbridge, delayed by about the same amount. Our climb up the Mendips proceeded without mishap, still with wall-to-wall sunshine and enough snow to create a pristine landscape but not deep enough to bury the running rails. At Bath our train left for Bristol just 40 minutes late behind a Hymek diesel.

With the sun setting in a clear sky and the snow cover still complete, temperatures were dropping rapidly. We took the first southbound train, the 15.20 stopper to Templecombe, which left more or less on time behind Standard class 5 No.73068. My notes show a delay of 20 minutes arriving at Evercreech Junction, with the 17.00 departure for Highbridge waiting for us in the centre road as usual. After that, however, things started to go really haywire, taking over 90 minutes to get from there to Templecombe, but without any explanation as to why. Approaching Templecombe, we passed the 16.13 Evercreech to Bournemouth train leaving two hours late, so that may have held us up.

Our train terminated at Templecombe and the timetable led us to expect, on a normal day, a wait of 35 minutes before the arrival of the 16.20 semi-fast from Bath. On that day, however, things were becoming far from normal. Instead of the 16.20 arriving at 17.38, the 16.35 stopper from Bath came in at 19.10 (51 minutes late) and the 16.20 behind it, leaving Templecombe with us on it at 19.30, one hour 45 minutes late, with Standard 4 No.76014 in charge.

By this time it was getting very cold indeed. We passed freight trains in the yards at Stalbridge and Sturminster Newton. The latter we saw at just before 20.00, a train that normally leaves Poole at 15.00! But our train also had its problems. Quite a few passengers were due to get off at Sturminster but most of the carriage doors had frozen up so several of them were unable to get out. The train left with furious passengers shouting from the windows and remonstrating later with the guard. By that time there was little he could do. The already late passengers had to continue onto Blandford and change onto the evening Bournemouth to Bath train. We later passed this train at Corfe Mullen so they would probably have had a further half hour to wait at Blandford!

We arrived back in Poole at 20.52, exactly two hours late. For me it had been a fascinating day's outing, but I fear that for many others it was a day to be rapidly forgotten!

9F No.92233 runs around the sharp curve and is about to pass over Towngate Street level crossing at Poole with an up train. (*Keith Barrett collection*)

BR class 2P No.40505 rounds the curve at Poole with a down train in 1952; a year later she was withdrawn from service. (*Keith Barrett collection*)

(*above left*) Driver Donald Beale ready to leave Branksome loco on BR Standard class 4 No.76012. Donald started on the S&D in 1919 and spent 47 years on the railway. (*Donald Beale collection*)

(*above right*) LMS Stanier 5MT No.44839 is the backdrop for Branksome railwaymen, c.1953. From left to right, passed fireman Steve Penny, cleaner Arthur Gover, steamraiser Charlie Merryfield and fireman Bill Harford. (*Bill Harford collection*)

(*below*) 7F No.53809 (now preserved) takes on water at Branksome shed in readiness for a return working to Bath on 26 July 1952. (*Keith Barrett collection*)

2P No.698 is waiting to leave Bournemouth West with an up passenger train. Note the 22A shed plate (Bristol Barrow Road) on the smokebox door. (*Keith Barrett collection*)

The driver and a member of the church pose beside 2P No.696 on shed at Bournemouth Central. On the right is King Arthur N15 class No.740 *Merlin*. (*Keith Barrett collection*)

Fireman Brian Bush (left) and driver William (Johnny) Walker. Johnny started on the S&D in 1921 at Bath Green Park and moved to Bournemouth in 1927. One of the most likeable enginemen on the whole of the S&D with always a story to tell. Johnny gave over 50 years service to the railway. Note the Cherry Blossom has been busy. (*Angela Holttum collection*)

(*right*) Bournemouth passenger guard Alf Metcalfe, one of the most respected guards on the whole S&D, a dedicated railwayman. In 1963 he retired after 49 years on the railway – will railwaymen ever give this length of service again? (*Ray Metcalfe collection*)

(*below*) Driver Den Norris (left) and fireman Robin Gould waiting to leave with the 15.40 Bournemouth-Bath train on a class 5 No.73052. (*Roy Miles collection*)

(*above*) Pylle Halt facing towards Evercreech Junction, c.1956. Porteress Betty Spiller recalls working here in the war years. On one occasion she started work at 10.00 and did not finish until 21.00. The only traffic she had all day was 50 rabbits for a customer in Crystal Palace, London. (*H.C.Casserley*)

(*left*) An unusual sight at Pylle Halt, giving an interesting view of the station building. A Bedford van has crashed alongside the road bridge carrying the A37. Hopefully nobody was injured. (*Vic Freak collection*)

South Western & Midland Railway Companies' Somerset & Dorset Joint Line.

(40?)

No. _____ _____ Station,

_____187

ADVICE OF INSURED PARCELS AND GOODS.

Consignee _____

Description _____

Declared Value _____

Amount paid for Insurance £ _____

The above has this day been forwarded by* _____ Train to your Station. If not to hand in due course, immediate enquiry must be made, and the case at once reported to your Superintendent or Goods Manager.

_____ Station Agent.

* Say here whether by " Passenger " or " Goods " Train.

(*left, above*) West Pennard station. In the good old days the Green family distributed their fine cheeses from here. Another company, W.T.Allen, brought barrels of cider to the station for delivery to their customers and there was always a jar for the porters. Some of the station's buildings are still in fine order today. (*Author's collection*)

(*left, below*) West Pennard signalbox had 23 levers and was situated at the end of the up platform. Bill Harris, Reg Biffin and Evelyn Curtis worked this signalbox. Miss Curtis always had a fine display of fresh flowers in the box, which was a delight to see. (*Keith Barrett collection*)

(*right*) Fireman Robin Gould has just exchanged tablets with West Pennard signalman Tom Salisbury on a crisp April day in 1964. (*Robin Gould collection*)

(*below*) On a fine day looking towards Glastonbury, 2P No.40563 enters West Pennard with a parcels train. The station looks in a tidy order and on the right is a post-war Hillman Minx. (*E.T.Gill/R.K.Blencowe collection*)

Guards' Signatures.

PARCELS WAY BILL.

I or Passenger Train traffic charged by weight at Parcels rates or otherwise, in quantities of LESS than 2 CWTS.

WEST PENNARD to _Kilburn_ Via _Coombe_

Departure _7/50_ o'clock Train _3_ day of _11_ 189 _8_

No.	Description.	NAME.	DESTINATION	Weight. lbs.	PAID ON. s. d.	TO PAY. £ s. d.	PAID. £ s. d.	THRO'. s. d.	Under-charge.	Over-charge.	Sender.
1	Bx	F. Hawke 42 Campagne Gdns		12			9				Ames

N.B.—The Guard of the Train must see that the entries on this Bill correspond with the Parcels delivered to and given up by him.

[40A.]

South Western & Midland Railway Companies' SOMERSET & DORSET JOINT LINE.

6

MILK WAY BILL.

No. _____

From **WEST PENNARD** to _Wimbledon Coombe_

Departure _6/15_ o'clock Train _6_ day of _Dec_ 189 _9_

No.	Description.	NAME.	DESTINATION.	Not exceeding. Gallons.	PAID ON. s. d.	TO PAY. £ s. d.	PAID. £ s. d.	Under-charged.	Sender.
2		Clark		3/18			3 9		Staff
1		Hornby		1/18			1 11		
1		Witt		18			1 11		
1		Sane		11			1 0		
1		Eakchff		0			1 1		
3		Frghs		3/12 1/16			4 7		Bod
1		Bey		1/18			1 11		Bod

162

Guards' Signatures.

PARCELS WAY BILL.

I or Passenger Train traffic charged by weight at Parcels rates or otherwise, in quantities of LESS than 2 CWTS.

WEST PENNARD to _Stourbridge_ Via _High_

Departure _10/40_ o'clock Train _22_ day of _42_ 189 _8_

No.	Description.	NAME.	DESTINATION	Weight. lbs.	PAID ON. s. d.	TO PAY. £ s. d.	PAID. £ s. d.	THRO'. s. d.	Under-charge.	Over-charge.	Sender.
1	Bx	Palmer		22			1 4				Farrant

N.B.—The Guard of the Train must see that the entries on this Bill correspond with the Parcels delivered to and given up by him.

(*left*) Parcels and Milk Way Bills, dating from 1898, showing traffic from West Pennard to parts of London via Templecombe and to Stourbridge via Highbridge.

Cemetery Lane Crossing in wintry conditions, between Glastonbury and West Pennard. The crossing keeper was Joyce Miles; her husband Eric was the signalman at Glastonbury. What a shame it has now disappeared for ever. (*Eric Miles*)

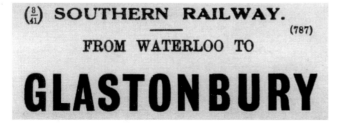

Guard Tom Mundy gives the right away at Glastonbury to driver John Dray on Ivatt 2MT No. 41248, working the 16.05 Templecombe–Highbridge train. (*Keith Barrett collection*)

Glastonbury and Street station looking towards Ashcott. It was an impressive station with large canopies and an elaborate covered footbridge linking the two platforms. With a bustling goods yard and passengers to look after, staff Sam Bailey, Bill Milton, Fred Lester, Ted Cook, Hugh Durston and Ron Snook were always kept busy. (*Keith Barrett collection*)

From left to right, guard Cyril Cox, driver Ronald (Chummy) Andrews and fireman George Stent are seen alongside Collett No.3206 prior to departure from Glastonbury goods yard in 1962. (*R.E.Toop*)

(*right*) Driver John Dray on the footplate of Ivatt 2MT No.41248 enjoying a leisurely chat with Glastonbury signalman Colin Gregory. Colin's dog seems to be interested in something in the cab. (*Rodney Scovell*)

(*below*) From left to right, guard Francis Packer, driver Clarence Rawles and fireman Mike Lewis stand in front of Collett 2251 class 3MT No.3218 on a cold winter's day at Glastonbury yard. Francis, known to everybody as Frank, started as a porter at Midsomer Norton in 1918 and gave over 48 years of loyal service to the S&D. (*Francis Packer collection*)

Ashcott

The S&D was known as a family railway. At Ashcott and Meare station on the Somerset levels it was exactly that. The station had a single platform on the down side, a ground frame with a booking office and waiting room situated next to the station house where Archie and Edna Atwell lived.

In the 1960s they worked the station between them carrying out all tasks which included issuing tickets, opening and closing the crossing gate, as well as platform duties. Archie performed all the shunting in the single siding; most of the traffic at that time was from the local peat works and cattle from nearby farms.

In the 1950s at the age of four, their daughter Janet had her first taste of railways. Archie's first job on the S&D was as a porter at Edington Junction; he would put Janet on the crossbar of his auto cycle and take her to work with him. In her early teens Janet had many a footplate ride on the early evening train to Evercreech Junction with her husband to be, fireman Tony Rossiter. The family was well known up and down the line by staff and customers. For them it wasn't just a job; it was a way of life, which they thoroughly enjoyed. Communities were built around the railway and this certainly was the case at Ashcott.

Tony and Janet now live in a bungalow on the Ashcott station site and still have fond memories of those happy and idyllic days, which are reflected in these family photographs of the railway.

A fine picture on a bright summer's day of the stationmaster's house at Ashcott. Note the BR fire bucket, water can, porter's barrow and truck for passengers' luggage.

(left) Archie and Edna Atwell outside the station house where they lived and worked. The flowers look stunning.

(below) Edna, standing in front of the level crossing gates at Ashcott, on a windy day.

(below) Janet Rossiter, (nee Atwell), with their pet dog Spot standing in front of the ten-lever ground frame.

Somerset & Dorset Rly. Jt. C'tee.
PRIVILEGE TICKET.
Available for One including Day of issue
Issued subject to the conditions (a) on the
Privilege Ticket Order & (b) on the back hereof.
Ashcott to
Via
Third Class
0065
0065

(right) Ashcott children at their home station on a day out to Burnham-on-Sea. Two sets of family twins, 2nd and 6th left Brian and Jean, 3rd and 4th left Margaret and Maureen Squire. Others in the picture are Chris, Gordon, Colin and Trevor Foster.
(*Maureen Thick, née Squire, collection*)

(*above*) Collett 2251 class 0-6-0 No.2219 on a local from Highbridge, stands in the platform at Ashcott station in 1962. (*C.L.Caddy*)

Fireman Tony Rossiter (left) and driver Les Warren look out from the cab of Collett No.2219.

Signalman Walter Cook looks out of Shapwick signalbox. In season with the rhyne nearby, the box was inundated with mayflies.
(*John Cook collection*)

Bulldog 3F No.43194, built at Derby in 1896, leaves Shapwick tender-first with a local for Evercreech Junction. (*Keith Barrett collection*)

Looking towards Edington, signalman Bill Vowles exchanges tablets with the fireman of a goods train headed by Ivatt 2MT No.41208 at Shapwick station.
(*Fred Vowles collection*)

An evocative S&D branch scene at Edington Burtle with Collett 2251 No.3210 on a stopper for Evercreech in 1962. (*E.T.Gill/R.K.Blencowe collection*)

Ivatt 2MT No.41307 passing Edington Burtle station with a freight train for Highbridge. The station was originally known as Edington Road, and became Edington Junction in 1890 when it formed the junction for Bridgwater. When the Bridgwater branch closed in 1952 it became Edington Burtle. *(Maurice Cook collection)*

3F No.43218 darting away with a single coach from Edington Junction heading for Bridgwater North. (*Keith Barrett collection*)

Footplate man Norman Cook posing for the camera at Edington Junction on 1P No.58086 after bringing in the 15.55 from Bridgwater North on 11 June 1952. (*Francis Pook*)

Edington Junction signalbox between 1890 and 1900. Could it be the 1890 opening of the Bridgwater railway, especially with all the railway dignitaries on the veranda? Note the gentleman on the right; is that a box camera in his hand? (*SDRT collection*)

The Parsons family at Edington: (*left*) at 14 years of age Fred Parsons started on the S&D as a junior porter at Edington Junction in 1941. He worked at every station between Highbridge and Evercreech including the Bridgwater and Wells branch lines. (*Fred Parsons collection*)

(*below right*) Porteress Evelyn Parsons coming off duty at Edington Junction in 1942. Her brothers Fred and Percy also worked as porters at the same station. (*Percy Parsons collection*)

(*below left*) Percy Parsons ready for the late turn at Edington Junction in 1940. He was 50 years a railwayman, many of them on the branch. (*Percy Parsons collection*)

Bill Vowles sets off from his home to take on his duties as a porter at Edington Junction in the 1950s; later he became a signalman at Shapwick. (*Fred Vowles collection*)

Father and son in front of Chilton Drove crossing gate in the 1930s. Hubert Rice was a porter at Edington, his son John started as a porter at the same station and then went on to the footplate. John's mother Agnes was the crossing keeper here. (*John Rice collection*)

Everything looks still and quiet at Edington Burtle station. Porter Archie Atwell's Morris 8 stands next to the station wall. (*Tony Rossiter collection*)

Armstrong class 4F No.44560 is passing the milk factory at Bason Bridge with a Southern Wanderer Rail Tour. This loco was introduced in 1922 and built for the S&D to Midland design. *(E.T.Gill/R.K.Blencowe collection)*

The driver drops off empty water churns at Bason Bridge, while his GWR 0-6-0 No.3206 is simmering gently in the midday sun in 1962. (*R.E.Toop*)

Southern and London Midland and Scottish Railway Companies

SOMERSET AND DORSET RAILWAY JOINT COMMITTEE.

EGGS

WITH CARE.

The permanent way party erecting a new platform at Highbridge in November 1932 to replace the original wooden structure. The gentleman second from the right with dark overcoat and trilby hat is lookout flagman William Slocombe. *(SDRT collection)*

Ivatt class 2MT No.41307 with a passenger train at Highbridge bay platform. The loco carries an S&D crest on the front buffer beam and could be a special. Driver Bill May is walking towards the gents. *(Maurice Cook collection)*

Driver Maurice Cook started on the S&D as a caller up and bar boy in 1934. He followed in his father Ernest's footsteps, who was also a driver at Highbridge. Maurice spent 32 years working on the branch. (*Maurice Cook collection*)

Driver Walt Jeans (left) and fireman David Young enjoy a rest at Highbridge loco cabin, before taking the 14.20 passenger train back to Templecombe. Note the old-fashioned grate and railwayman's friend, the metal tea can. (*Trevor Jeans collection*)

Driver Harry Pearce sets off for work at Highbridge on his bike. Harry was one of the senior drivers on the branch for many years. (*Joyce Bell collection*)

From left to right, wagon examiner Reg Bishop, driver Ronald (Chummy) Andrews and fireman Tom Carp pose for this picture at Highbridge in the 1950s. (*SDRT collection*)

Driver Charlie King on the running plate of Collett 2251 No.3218 on his last working day on the S&D. He is seen here shaking hands with one of his workmates, driver Ronald (Chummy) Andrews. To the left of Charlie is fireman Tony Rossiter. On the far left are fitter's mate Cyril (Captain) Burrows and fitter Phil Owen. (*Tony Rossiter collection*)

Frank Jones looks out of the window of Highbridge East C box. It controlled access to the locomotive depot, the single line eastwards and a short length of double track westwards. (*Trevor Jeans collection*)

Driver Bill May stands next to Ivatt class 2MT No.41249 (83G Templecombe) at Highbridge. Bill, an expert railwayman, spent over 45 years on the S&D. (*John Lock collection*)

Vulcan 0-4-4T No.53, built in 1885 and withdrawn in 1930, stands at Highbridge with three engine crew looking on. (*Keith Barrett collection*)

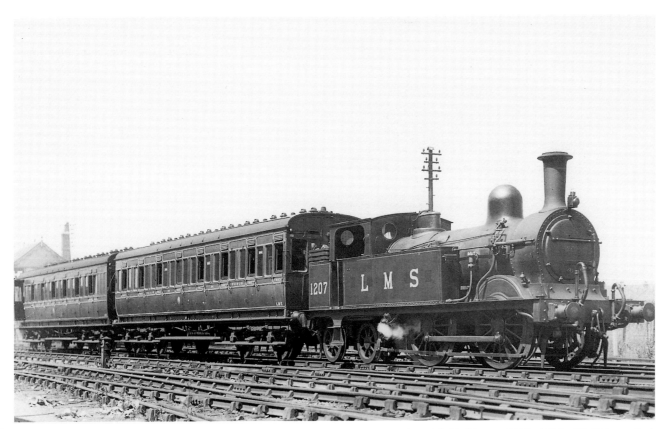

Johnson Tank S&D No.31, now sporting LMS No.1207, with a two-coach train at Highbridge on 5 July 1930. (*H.C.Casserley*)

On 30 May 1929 4-4-0 No.18, built at Derby in 1891, looks very clean and ready for traffic as she stands at Highbridge yard. (*H.C.Casserley*)

Francis Pook

In the 1940s I lived within three-quarters of a mile of the S&D branch line at Chilton upon Polden and have many memories of it during its last 12 years before sadly it closed. One could say it was almost an obsession.

My ear was always alert for the sound of the trains; I would rush to the line side to see a passing Johnson 0-4-4T or later a 3F on its way to Bridgwater. My nearest vantage points were Landshire Bridge on Chilton bank and the Stone End crossing area.

When awaiting the 11.05 or its equivalent from Cossington to Bridgwater in the wartime, late time being usual, one knew when the branch train should be on its way up, because the connecting Evercreech-Burnham train came into view in the distance, heading towards Huntspill. The Bridgwater train emerged from a deep cutting on a left-hand bend, a column of steam appearing just before the engine. Steam was shut off as the train rolled along the short embankment and into the station.

Cossington station opened in 1890. It had a platform on the up side of the single line and a stone building for the station facilities; for such a small station it boasted a stationmaster's house. I remember that in the days when there was a canopy at the station the buildings were painted in SR green and cream livery. Soon after a re-paint the canopy was taken down, whether for safety or to save paint, we did not know, but it was a loss to the building. The booking hall always seemed to smell of disinfectant. To a small boy there was excitement in knowing that to this quiet place would soon arrive a noisy puffer. I bought my first ticket there from porter George Pepperall; an explanation was required as to why I should ask for a half return to Bridgwater when I wanted to return to Cossington! After a short time Mr. Pepperall understood what I meant and gave me my ticket. At Bridgwater I had my first ride on an engine; driver George Yard invited me up on to the footplate with parental permission. I held on fast and we went out and back on the first half of the running round operation. That friendly driver always had a chat with us at the station and would whistle if we waved from the line side.

I recall on another occasion in the booking hall at Bridgwater, there was an enormous circular saw of about seven foot diameter, the teeth suitably protected with battens and destined for one of the timber yards nearby. There was a fair amount of shunting at Bridgwater before the departure of the early afternoon down train and on one occasion I saw a second engine working in the yard, giving an impression of much activity on the line, an unusual sight.

At Bawdrip Halt, a mile or so from Cossington, when standing at the halt, a down train often crept backwards and had to be checked. The re-start was usually fairly strong up Cossington bank, but then the regulator was closed for a few seconds while the driver notched up. The train would make an economical rather than a brisk climb under the bridges and into Cossington station. Local farmers used the trains as a rough and ready timepiece, especially when down the moor, milking, ditching or haymaking.

Another station on the branch was Edington Junction; later, after the Bridgwater branch closed, it was called Edington Burtle. This could be busy at times, with the branch train arriving at the down platform, and then going across to the bay. A longish goods train, stretching back towards Catcott crossing, would be standing off, waiting to cross a down passenger train on the Burnham-Evercreech line. Water churns to supply crossing keepers at Catcott, Huntspill, Chilton Drove and Stone End were filled at Edington station. They were taken out on the running plate of the engine. Hot water from the engine's boiler could be supplied to the keepers for the weekly wash or to fill the tin bath. A hand bell, rung by signalmen Harry Sweetland or Tom Mogg for the crossing gates to be opened will be remembered by most people who used the station. One dark evening, as we were coming back from London, the Edington stationmaster Tom Pugh seemed displeased as he muttered 'Oh, they're racing again'. Occasionally the two westbound trains, one going to Bridgwater and the other to Burnham, were given the right away simultaneously. The two drivers were tempted to compete along the few hundred yards of track before their ways diverged. From the locomotives came a loud barking and up went a fountain of red-hot cinders much to Mr. Pugh's annoyance. Trains to Burnham ran along to the far end of the platform, instead of stopping under the canopy, as they should have for travellers' convenience. An easier exchange of the key at the signalbox was probably the reason for this. I heard driver Norman Cook exclaiming on arrival at Edington with a mixed train, that he had only just managed to pull away from Bawdrip with his 1P using full gear; 'She's as weak as a robin' he said.

In the Second World War the Burtle platoon of the home guard, composed partly of railwaymen, used the station for its defence locality and the stationmaster's office as its headquarters. My father was the platoon commander. Edington signalman Harry Sweetland, who once showed me around the signalbox, was Cpl. First Aid in the platoon; other S&D members were Walt Clark, Hubert Rice, Percy Parsons and Walter Cook. One afternoon a German bomb fell just east of the level crossing gates, damaging the point work of the passing loop. I heard the explosion and saw the smoke from Chilton.

After the war the station received some repairs and was to have been re-painted in WR colours of brown and yellow but, apart from some patching, never was.

My father told me of seeing passenger stock going to Bridgwater for the ten-coach 'Bridgwater Allotment Holders' excursion train, also extra goods traffic in connection with the Bath and West show. A letter he sent to me when I was away at school, dated 27 May 1946, told of an interesting incident on the branch. The last goods train from Bridgwater to Edington Junction had killed two of Mr. Arthur Coombes' cows and hurt the bull so badly that he had to be slaughtered. The bull was tethered in a field next to the line but broke loose, got onto the line and the heifers followed.

My recollection of the last day of passenger train working on the Bridgwater branch, Saturday 29 November 1952, was of a very cold and wet day. Snow fell in the morning, turning to sleet in the afternoon and rain in the evening – a very sad and depressing day for the villagers who used the railway and of course for the S&D staff who, since 1890, had worked the line.

My round trips that day were from Cossington to Bridgwater, then on the last train to Edington, and finally back to Cossington. Whilst waiting for the last up departure on the branch a small group of us stood

Ticket issued on the last day of passenger working on the Bridgwater branch, 29 November 1952.

in the booking hall listening to those with long memories of the line, telling their tales. One I recall was Bridgwater railwayman Will Locke, a dedicated S&D man. Then came the last connection, a down train on the run to Evercreech Junction – empty. Then after the porter's familiar but never to be repeated call 'Edington Junkshin, Edington Junkshin, change for Cuzzit'n and Bri-jwad'r', we boarded the final passenger train, with Johnson 0-4-4T No.58073 in charge, and driver Charlie King, relief driver George Brooks acting as fireman and guard Jack Alford. No one there could forget that departure, punctuated all the way out to Chilton Drove Crossing by the bangs of dozens of detonators. Crossing keeper Agnes Rice and her husband Hubert, a porter at Edington, were at their front door with lamps, waving as we passed. Not wishing to return home by bus, I alighted at Cossington, thus missing the very end, but able to watch and listen as the train steamed away into the darkness, before sadly walking home.

During the two years of goods only operations a man working near the line told me of a partial derailment of an engine while shunting Cossington siding. 'The whole Highbridge breakdown gang turned up', he said: 'There were darned near enough of 'em to lift the engine back by hand'. No doubt some overtime pay was to be had.

The railway I knew was a quiet and friendly branch line, loved by many and sadly missed when it was closed.

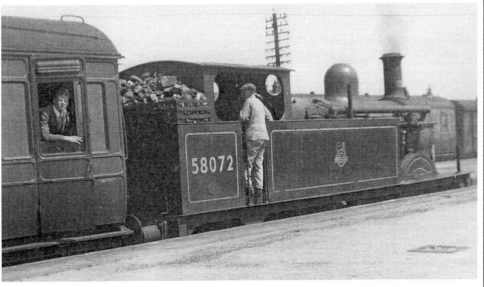

Francis Pook has just boarded the afternoon passenger train at Highbridge in the 1950s, headed by 1P No.58072, with a full bunker, for this trip to Templecombe. (*Francis Pook collection*)

Staff pose in this early photo of Highbridge carriage and wagon works. c.1900. In the background a bogie coach is being built. (*SDRT collection*)

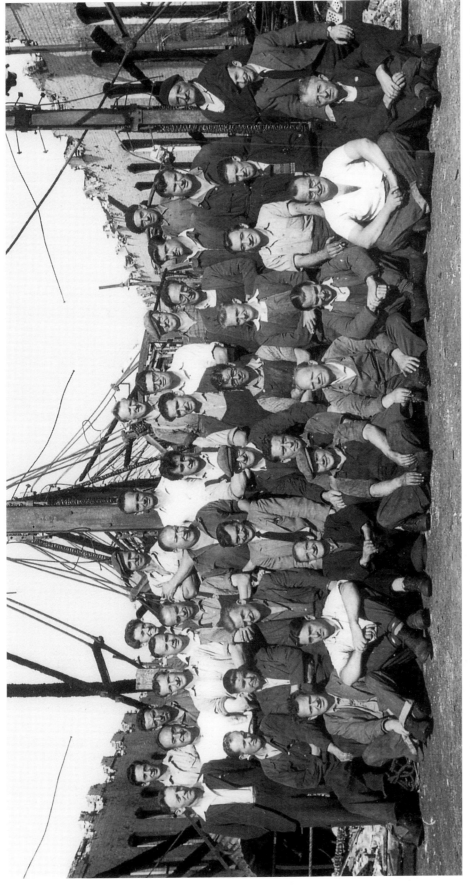

The old wagon and carriage works in Highbridge was being used to repair covered wagons until 1955 when unfortunately the building was destroyed by fire. In the ruins, the staff that worked there had this last picture taken. Back row, from left to right, Ken Clapp, Archie Taylor, George Thomas, Bert Masterman, Bob Hooper, Walt Bishop, Ted Woodward; third row, Bert Warren, Doug Holley, Jeff Thresher, Ken Denman, Ray Cook, Harold Taylor, Cliff Heal, Arthur Driscoll, Dick Connelly, Frank Smith, Wilf Haggett, Mervyn Bamsey, Ernie Cock, Ern Goddard; second row, Ern Collins, Jack Fisher, Reg Fisher, Larry Storey, Bert Fackrell, Les Diment, Ken Ford, Sam Gregory, Cyril Dyer, Bill Banwell; front row, Les Brown, Walt Bennett, Jack Ward, Mick Clare, Ted Clare, Les Jones, Dick Coulson, John Thorne, Syd Pugsley. *(Mary Draper collection)*

An early 1920s picture of over 180 members of staff at Highbridge works

ow, 12th from the left, is apprentice Sam Lane. (*G.Balcombe collection*)

With platform maintenance taking place at Burnham-on-Sea 1P 0-4-4T No.1370 (22E) gets ready to depart. (*Keith Barrett collection*)

On a warm sunny day 1P No.58086 leaves Burnham-on-Sea station with a down local. (*Keith Barrett collection*)

Well-known porter Hugh Berryman at Burnham-on-Sea in the 1920s. (*Joan Fisher collection*)

(*below*) 3F No.43248 has just arrived with an excursion train at Burnham-on-Sea on August Bank Holiday 1954. (*Francis Pook*)

Avonside 0-4-4T No.10 at Burnham-on-Sea, with *The Queens Hotel* (formerly *The Reed Arms*) in the background in the 1920s. (*Keith Barrett collection*)

Burnham-on-Sea pier, the end of the line for the S&D. The main running rails were used by shipping to load and unload cargo. Burnham's lifeboat also used the rails until 1930. In the background is a small ship, probably a collier laden with South Wales coal. (*Peter McGhie collection*)

No.58072 is about to leave Bridgwater North on 5 September 1952. On the right-hand side there are a number of sacks of coal, winter is on its way. (*H.C.Casserley*)

Signalman Dennis Ashill has come out of his warm signalbox to take this picture of arctic conditions looking towards Bridgwater station. Who would like to be on the footplate, tender-first, going across the Somerset levels on a day like this? The signalbox had 17 levers and was situated next to the level crossing at the Drove. (*Dennis Ashill*)

(*above*) Scottie 0-6-0 No.51, built by the Vulcan foundry in 1884, on Bridgwater shed. This photo must have been taken before 1925 as she was withdrawn in November of that year.
(*Keith Barrett collection*)

(*right*) Johnson class 1P No.58072 is about to pass over the Drove Crossing before entering Bridgwater North station.
(*Dennis Ashill*)

Horace Pople accepting a barometer after 51 years service on the railway (many on the S&D). In the group, from left to right, are Ern Whitehead, Wilf Saunders (stationmaster), Fred Allen, Horace Pople, Reg Carter, Graham Hughes, not known, Bert Lake, not known and Will Locke. (*Will Locke collection*)

Porter Gilbert Ashill in the goods depot at Bridgwater sitting in an easy chair given to him by his workmates after 47 years on the railway, mostly on the S&D. His colleagues in this photo include Ralph Venning, Jack Warren, J.Manning, Herbie Parker, Horace Venning, Bill Heal, Bill Lush, Johnny Collard, Bert Williams, D.Crocker, Joyce Fear, S.Alford, Peter Criddle and Charlie Fuller. (*Dennis Ashill collection*)

Yes, a photograph of Bawdrip Halt, taken on 18 March 1952, eight months before closure. The platform was of SR concrete design, with a small shelter. This Halt was the lifeblood for the villagers, as it enabled them to do their weekly shopping in Bridgwater. (*S.C.Townroe/R.K.Blencowe collection*)

Cossington station, photographed c.1912, was opened in 1890. It had a single platform and a ground frame that operated the single siding. The greystone buildings housed the booking office, waiting rooms and stationmaster's house. (*Will Locke collection*)

London and South Western Ry.

787

FROM WATERLOO TO

COSSINGTON

(*left*) George Perkins on his home made three-wheeler. George lost a leg in a railway accident in the 1880s and made this bike so he could get to work as a porter at Wincanton and later as the stationmaster at Polsham. His daughter Gladys is in the background. (*Evelyn Perkins collection*)

(*below*) Polsham Halt opened in 1861 and closed in 1951. The station was the only stop between Glastonbury and Wells. In the distance a loco can be seen, bunker-first, with some wagons, c.1950. (*Stations.UK collection*)

A very rare photo of Polsham Halt, probably taken between 1900 and 1910. The three gentlemen, from left to right, are most likely to be the stationmaster, station porter and maybe a local farmer. (*Gordon Lee collection*)

Guard Bob Fry indulging in a spot of shunting with the Wells branch train on the goods shed road at Priory Road. Driver Henry Fowler is in charge of the Johnson 0-4-4T No.1303. (*Keith Barrett collection*)

Home Guard

In the Second World War, staff on the S&D, like many others across Britain, became members of their Local Defence Volunteers (Home Guard). Many good-humoured stories are recalled about the Home Guard, but it must be remembered that many hundreds lost their lives whilst on duty and in Somerset at least 22 members were killed. The photographs in this section depict railwaymen and others who joined the Home Guard and did their bit in defence of their country.

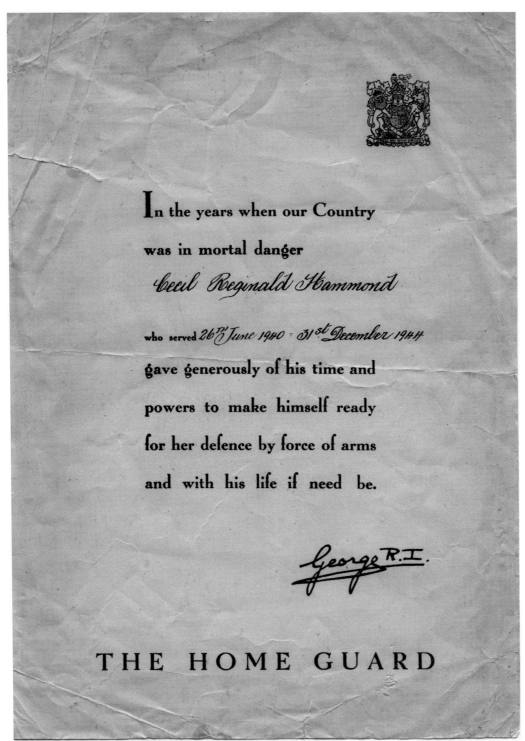

The certificate awarded to the author's grandfather, Cecil Hammond, for his service in the Home Guard.

George Dyer

In my twilight years I often reflect back to my youthful days as a fireman at Templecombe. They were without doubt the happiest days of my life. The comradeship, life-long friends and humour that existed everywhere on the S&D can still be found when we all meet up for reunions.

I started as a cleaner in 1940 at Templecombe with my best mate Bert Collins and as it was wartime I rapidly progressed to fireman. Other S&D men who were there at that time were Vic Prior, Walt Jeans, Pat Gawler, Leo Elkins, Eric Elford and Stan Good.

One journey I shall never forget happened in April 1942 when I was in Bath sidings with my driver Fred Scott on 7F 53807. We had 56 wagons of ammunition for Blandford; they were all marked with the red label, which we knew was distinctive for high explosives. Suddenly and without warning German planes were overhead and bombs were dropping from the sky, followed quickly by machine-gunning nearby. As Bath was in a basin the noise was horrendous; the reality of what was happening was truly frightening especially with the ammo behind us. Scotty, my driver, shouted at me to run to the signalbox which was a couple of 100 yards away and urgently ask the bobby for the right away. I have never run so fast to that signalbox, all I could hear was the explosions in the background as I ran up the steps to the box. On informing the signalman that we had enough explosives to wipe out part of Bath, which would cause many casualties, including him, he got the message. I scampered back to the 7F, which was silhouetted by the backdrop of fires in the distance. On reaching the cab the signal was lowered, but we had a problem. After sitting in the sidings for some time our fire was now just a little red glow with white ash on top, and we were quickly trying to maintain steam for an immediate departure. We had our glow sheets up as we called them, around the cab, making sure no light was showing through. Scotty was opening the firebox door as I shovelled the coal in. He then shut the door tight as I got more coal down from the tender. Within a very short time we were on the move, looking back at our rake of 56 wagons with its deadly cargo and our guard in his van; we were glad to leave the mayhem, but our thoughts were with the people of Bath who were under this bombardment of terror. Our 7F wasn't letting us down, picking up speed as we made our way out of Bath to Devonshire and Combe Down Tunnels. It was the first time we had ever looked forward to going into those dark holes. As we went through Midford at speed the signalman must have thought we were a ghost train as we flashed by in complete darkness. We made Blandford without further incident and I must admit I was glad to get home alive and well.

On one occasion I was on yard duties at Templecombe on a lovely sunny day. Suddenly the call went out: 'Train on fire'; staff came running from all directions. The train came to a stop and we immediately saw that it was a down special troop train from Bath, but not knowing its destination we assumed it was destined for Blandford camp. A large parcels van was on fire due to a hot box; the van was uncoupled and moved to a safer distance away from the other carriages. The doors were opened and revealed quite a fire in the van; the contents inside were kitbags and cases. We rushed about and got some long rakes that were carried on tenders (a useful tool when managing an engine's firebox). Many of us set to work pulling all the kitbags out to the track side; it was quite a pitiful sight to see the troops under orders not to leave the train as we were raking all their possessions out of the burning van. Fire hoses were set up from Templecombe depot to extinguish the fire. Fortunately many kitbags and cases were saved from the fire by the Templecombe staff.

I would like to relate a story, which includes humour and trauma. I was in the Templecombe Home Guard 22 Devon regiment. After reading Alan Hammond's last book *Life on the Somerset & Dorset Railway*, in which there was a photo of the Bath Green Park Home Guard and the foreword of the book was written by Bill Pertwee of *Dad's Army* fame, this brought back vivid memories of my first night on guard duties. I reported for duty feeling rather proud in my new battledress, with highly polished toecaps, complete with greatcoat, gas mask and tin hat; I was now ready for anything when the church bells rang, to go on parade. My sergeant in charge, Bernard Dyer the depot superintendent, was still in his railway clothes with his bowler hat perched on his head. We all went into an office with little furniture, none if I remember rightly. Sergeant Dyer picks up a rifle, which was a Canadian Ross and says, 'Now look, this is a very dangerous weapon and must be treated as such'. He now proceeds to explain the loading and safety of the weapon. 'Firstly you open the breech bolt action, and then you get a clip of five rounds of ammunition.' At that moment I interrupted him and said: 'Are you going to use the clips above the fireplace'; these were dummy bullets with the same cartridge case, but identified by blue-painted wooden bullets. In his hand he had a clip of five-nickel bullets and they were live. He ignored me and proceeded to push the five rounds down on the W spring. He pushed the bolt home with one round up the spout; I heard the click of the bolt going home and then these words: 'This weapon is rendered harmless by putting the safety catch on'. Unfortunately the safety catch was off when he squeezed the trigger. At the precise moment when the rifle was discharged Ken Anderson the deputy superintendent entered the room carrying a metal tray with teapot and cups. Sergeant Dyer was standing at the side of the fireplace that had a flagstone hearth; I was standing in front of it, but fortunately to the side of where the muzzle of the rifle was facing. As Mr. Anderson entered, instead of hearing the metallic click of the firing pin going home there was a massive explosion of the rifle's discharge. The rifle shot out of Sergeant Dyer's hands with the recoil. The tray and contents went up in the air and crashed to the floor, Mr. Anderson crumpled to the ground. Sergeant Dyer tilted his bowler hat to the back of his head and was in a state of shock. The office was now full of depot staff who heard the explosion. Mr. Anderson was hit in the groin area and fragments of the burst bullet sent particles of nickel, lead and flagstone flying in all directions. I knew I had not got off scot-free because my face was peppered with fine particles of debris. Naturally the priority was Mr. Anderson who was put in Sergeant Dyer's Morris Minor and taken to Templecombe Merthyr Guest Hospital. During this time, after I had consumed two Woodbines, I found that my left foot felt wet and sloppy and I found that I had a tear in my new uniform. Further examination revealed a gash on my left knee and I was sent to the local hospital. I still bear the scar today. Naturally the military were informed and statements made for a full enquiry. Mr. Anderson recovered after a spell in hospital and no more was heard of the incident except in the messroom where it continued for many a day.

A funny tale concerned a real S&D character, Art Hatcher, whose son Gordon joined the S&D in 1943. Gordon recalls that his father was also a member of the platoon and enjoyed nothing better than a pint of Somerset scrumpy with his workmates. One Sunday morning they had a battle with the Parachute brigade over at the local woods. On the stroke of 12 o'clock, which was opening time, his father surrendered to the enemy and was taken to the *Royal Hotel*, which was being used as a prison for captured prisoners. He was enjoying a drink and fraternising with the enemy as members of the platoon were brought in with scratches and blood pouring from their faces. Gordon also remembers when his father was on the parade ground; he was always out of step with the other members of the platoon, hopping from one foot to another.

On another occasion we went on weapon training, the weapon being called the Northover Projector which was used to propel a mortar bomb. We were in this field, with a herd of cows in the corner, well out of harm's way, or so we thought. Unfortunately one dead-eyed dick placed the missile within a few feet of these innocent creatures and this caused a mini stampede; the farmer was not amused. One bright spark in the platoon said: 'Ah well, the farmer won't have milk tomorrow, he'll have butter'. Some members of the platoon I recall were Bert Rendle, Cecil Gillman, George Morley, Vic Prior, Percy Hobbs, Fritz Lawrence, Ray Stokes and Norman Light. Happy days.

Being wartime, food was very scarce and everyone was after what they could get. Driver Jimmy Good was given a couple of live ducks at Branksome, so how could he get them back to Templecombe without anyone knowing about it? With the help of his fireman Art Hatcher they put them in the water tank of their class 3F tender engine. Unfortunately on the journey back the water level went down and the injectors started to play up which led to a partial injector failure. Arriving at Templecombe the engine was taken out of service. On examination the sieve that protected the tank from leaves and other debris was covered in the dead duck feathers, as was the tender. A packet of Woodbines was passed to the fitter and everything was hushed up.

When Bert Collins and I moved to Saltley for promotion, the training and work experience we gained on the S&D stood us in good stead for anywhere on the railway network. For instance my first handover to a relief crew was the same as the S&D. Footplate brushed and hosed down, gauge glasses cleaned, boiler front wiped down with, hopefully, the water gauge showing $3/4$ full and fire in good nick. My mate Bert said to me: 'They won't do that for you here' and sure enough they didn't. As far as I was concerned this was the way of the S&D and I was sticking to it, which I did throughout my railway career.

Burtle Home Guard, c.1943. From left to right, Walter Clark, Nelson Moxey, Norman Moxey, Frank Lee, Hubert Rice, Charlie Sandford, Alan Moxey (junior), Victor Leigh, Ralph Pollard, Alan Moxey (senior), Wilfred Parsons, Tom Fisher, Ivor Bell, Captain John Pook, Bill Smith, Roland Norris, Tom Willis, Walter Cook, Edward Cox, Charlie Tratt, Arnold Tucker, Victor Pollard, Frank Vowles. *(Percy Parsons collection)*

18-year-old porter Percy Parsons on Home Guard duty at Edington in 1940. (*Percy Parsons collection*)

(*below*) Templecombe Railway Home Guard (known as 22 Devon Regiment). Some of the members of the platoon are seen here on the loading dock at Templecombe station. From left to right, Fred Hopkins, Cecil Gillman, Pete Morgan, Fred Rendle and Harry Hopkin. (*Ian Matthews collection*)

Members of the Highbridge Railway Home Guard. From left to right, Ern Cook, Maurice Cook, George Wheadon and Victor Newman. (*Maurice Cook collection*)

Members of the Highbridge Railway Home Guard. Back row, from left to right, Tom Bass, not known; front row, Harry Biffin, not known, Mark Hawkins. (*Reg Biffin collection*)

Glastonbury Railway Home Guard. Back row, from left to right, Wally Vincent (lorry driver), Reg Whitcombe (porter), Harold Heard (ganger), Stan Turner (lorry driver), Ted Billet (lorry driver), not known, Ern Napper (checker), not known; front row, Herbie Francis (permanent way), not known, Guy Parsons (porter), Reg Cox (Captain, permanent way), Les Carter (ganger), Fred Milton (ganger), Charlie Ham (lorry driver). (*Geoffrey Wilson collection*)

Templecombe Home Guard, (known as the Somerset's). Back row, from left to right, Albie Newman, Reg Newman, Jim Hatchley, Sid Brown, Len Lewis, Jim Hawkins, Vic Whitlock, Doug Maybee; middle row, Peter Sherston, Dick King, Fred Bennett, not known, B.Collins, not known, Dick Bennett, Ivor King, not known, Charlie Hawkins, Alex Appleby; front row, Charlie Hoare, John Dukes, not known, George Polly, George Robinson, Mr. Eager, Mr. Getlift, John Hazzard, not known, Frank Saywell. (*J.Hawkins collection*)

Index

Nutland, Ken 63

Osborne, Jack 72
Owen, Phil 128

Packer, Frank 107
Padfield, Frank 52
Parker, Herbie 145
Parsons, Albert 11
Parsons, Evelyn 118
Parsons, Fred 118
Parsons, Guy 156
Parsons, Percy 133, 154
Parsons, Peter 118
Parsons, Wilfred 153
Pearce, Harry 127
Penny, Joe 86
Penny, Steve 95
Pepperall, George 132
Perkins, George 147
Perkins, Gladys 147
Perry, Ken 63
Pitman, Fred 16
Pitt, Oscar 16-17, 21
Pitt, Sid 81
Pitt, Tony 11, 12, 20, 21
Pollard, Ralph 153
Pollard, Victor 153
Polly, George 157
Pook, Francis 132-133
Pook, John 153
Poole, Emily 46, 47
Poore, Den 49
Pope, Arthur (Giant) 80, 86
Pople, Horace 144
Powis, Colin 11
Prince, Jeff 16-17
Prior, Vic 151, 152
Puckett, Doug 62
Pugh, Tom 132
Pugsley, Syd 135

Rallison, Norman 49
Rawles, Bill 50
Rawles, Clarence 107
Reakes, Michael 40
Reed, Bert 46
Rendle, Bert 152
Rendle, Dick 64, 67
Rendle, Fred 154
Reynolds, Bev 13
Reynolds, Howard 13
Rhymes, Edward 83
Rice, Agnes 119, 133
Rice, Hubert 119, 133, 153
Rice, John 119
Richards, Arthur 52
Roberts (née Perry), Theresa 33
Robinson, George 157
Rogers, Walt 62
Rolls, Bert 72-73

Rood, Bert 156
Rossiter (née Atwell), Janet 108-109
Rossiter, Tony 108-110, 128
Russell, Bill 50
Ryall, Mike 13

Salisbury, Tom 101
Sandford, Charlie 153
Sanger, Dolly 69
Saunders, Harry 63
Saunders, Wilf 144
Sauqui, Howard 16
Savage, Percy 22
Sawyer, John 11-13
Saywell, Frank 157
Scott, Fred 151
Scovell, Harry 90
Scovell, Rodney 72
Scovell, Ted 66
Selman, Arthur 16-17
Sharlon, Reg 86
Shearn, Ron 47
Sherston, Peter 157
Simms, Maurice (Sam) 86
Simms, Ted 52
Slip, Tom 16-17
Slocombe, William 124
Smith, Bill 153
Smith, Cliff 39, 55
Smith, Edgar 40
Smith, Frank 135
Smith, Jack 16-17
Smith, Ron 13
Snook, Ron 105
Spiller, Betty 99
Spiller, Ron 63
Squire, Brian 109
Squire, Jean 109
Squire, Margaret 109
Squire, Maureen 109
Stacks, Bill 80
Staddon, Frank 13, 40, 46, 81
Staddon, Reg 13
Stainer, Sam 16-17
Stent, George 106
Stickley, Ern 86
Stokes, Ray 16, 65, 71, 152
Storey, Larry 135
Styling, Frank 69
Sweetland, Harry 132, 133

Talbot, Robert 30
Taylor, Archie 135
Taylor, Harold 135
Thomas, Clarence 67
Thorne, Dennis 50
Thorne, John 135
Thresher, Jeff 135
Tidball, Arthur 7, 17
Tooze, Mary 48
Tratt, Charlie 153

Trevor, George 16-17
Trowbridge, Frank 81
Trowbridge, Gerald 81
Tucker, Arnold 153
Tucker, George 32
Turner, Stan 156

Uphill, Fred 40
Upshall, Henry 80

Venner, Abe 46
Venning, Horace 145
Venning, Ralph 145
Vincent, Bill 80
Vincent, Wally 156
Vosper, Vic 62
Vowles, Bill 112, 119
Vowles, Frank 153

Waldron, Harry 10
Walker, William (Johnny) 97
Ward, Jack 135
Ward, Pete 49
Ware, Bernard 13, 22
Ware, Rose 48
Warren, Bert 135
Warren, Bill 46
Warren, Jack 145
Warren, Les 110
Warren, Walt 86
Watkins, Charlie 72, 81
Webb, Walt 66, 71
West, Ernie 63
Wheadon, George 155
Whitcombe, Reg 156
White, Sid 16-17
Whitehead, Ern 144
Whiting, Harold (Nobby) 86
Whitlock, Vic 157
Williams, Albert 12, 13, 46
Williams, Bert 145
Williams, Dave 13
Williams, George 81
Williams, Les 52
Williams, Roy 10, 16-17
Willis, Tom 153
Willshire, Ivor 16-17
Wilson, Alan 16-17
Wiltshire, Harry 22
Windsor, Dick 46
Withers, Clive 50
Woods, John 62
Woods, Walt 30
Woodward, Ted 135
Wort, Herbert 86

Yard, George 132
Young, Dave 62, 126